Eliminating Clutter
From Your Life

Eliminating Clutter
From Your Life

COMPILED AND EDITED BY

Susan Wright

A Citadel Press Book

Published by Carol Publishing Group

Carol Publishing Group Edition - 1994

A Citadel Press Book
Published by Carol Publishing Group
Citadel Press is a registered trademark of Carol Communications, Inc.
Editorial Offices: 600 Madison Avenue, New York, NY 10022
Sales & Distribution Offices: 120 Enterprise Avenue, Secaucus, NJ 07094
In Canada: Canadian Manda Group, P.O. Box 920, Station U, Toronto,
Ontario, M8Z 5P9, Canada
Queries regarding rights and permissions should be addressed to:
Carol Publishing Group, 600 Madison Avenue, New York, NY 10022

Manufactured in the United States of America
ISBN 0-8184-0544-9

15 14 13 12 11 10 9 8

Carol Publishing Group books are available at special discounts
for bulk purchases, for sales promotions, fund raising, or
educational purposes. Special editions can also be created to
specifications. For details contact: Special Sales Department,
Carol Publishing Group, 120 Enterprise Ave., Secaucus, NJ 07094

Library of Congress Cataloging-in-Publication Data

Eliminating clutter from your life / edited and compiled by
    Susan Wright.
    Includes index.
        First published as *The Learning annex guide to eliminating
        clutter from your life.*
  p. cm.
    1. House cleaning. Wright Susan.
  TX324.L43   1991
    648'.5-dc20
                                            91-7841
                                            CIP

Contents

1 | *How to Eliminate Clutter*

Do you have trouble throwing anything away?

No doubt about it—throwing away things you own involves a risk. Everyone thinks, "What if I need this object later, after it's too late?" and "What about the sentimental feelings involved?"

It's difficult, but here's one promise: you won't ever get rid of something that's absolutely essential to your life.

People who have problems with clutter are far too careful as it is. Certainly by following some general rules to free your life of the confusion of clutter, you don't run the risk of going berserk and throwing out those old family heirlooms. If you picked up this book or if someone bought it for you, then you have a problem with clutter. That's where this book can help.

The following tips are easy, and since you are not the organized type, you won't need to set up a schedule or tend to your clutter every day. Except for your desk and active work space, most of your clutter areas need to be examined only once or twice a year. Maintenance is easy when you learn how to stop clutter before it becomes a part of your life.

You'll be surprised. You'll feel more in control of your life once you gain control of the things you own.

This book is for you if:

- Your paperwork and files are a mess.
- You are surrounded by clutter and don't know why.
- You can never find a book in your library.
- The contents of your closets are a mystery.
- You are a confirmed collector.
- Your house is disorganized.
- You have no control over your time.

Why Do You Have Clutter in Your LIfe?

People save things because it gives them a sense of control over life. Usually it is a sign of insecurity, a way of holding onto something so that you know it will be there tomorrow. Recognize this and accept it.

The act of saving and collecting objects is not bad in itself, but it can replace your inner confidence with an outer manifestation of security. That, in turn, makes you more vulnerable. Your possessions can be lost, or stolen, or burned in a fire. If this thought terrifies you, then you should work on your need to keep things.

Just try throwing away some unneeded objects. You don't have to get rid of all your possessions, just one collection, one box of old clothes, a few books you never read, or knickknacks you hate. A safe thing to throw away is your three-year collection of old newspapers. Because something belongs to you doesn't mean you should keep it for the rest of your life.

As you cull the deadwood from your life, you will inevitably get a feeling of lightness and confidence. Without needless clutter and with your possessions safely organized, you don't have to spend as much time thinking about the objects in your life. Your possessions will stop getting in your way. And you will no longer have to deal with thoughts of "I should clean that closet" or "I'm so embarrassed that people see my house like this."

The Process of Eliminating Clutter

You must choose which possessions will remain with you and which ones should go. Don't try to grasp and hold on to everything. That simply keeps you from being in charge of your own life.

Pick one area of your house. Start in your front hall or den. If that seems too much for one day, then clear off a table. Work on one piece of furniture a day, and in a couple of weeks you'll have plowed through a whole houseful of clutter. You'll be able to see tangible results of your efforts, and it won't take long hours to get it all done.

Consider Each Object

Only two kinds of objects should be kept: (1) objects that are used, and (2) objects which are kept as mementos.

Pick up each object and ask yourself: Do I use this frequently? Seldom? Never? Throw it out if you use it once every couple of years. Keep only objects that you use.

Find something right now that you don't use. An old magazine, a clipping you were saving, a dust-covered jar or knickknack. Now throw it away.

If you have trouble, you're probably placing a false importance on the object. Don't attach sentiment to things simply because you own them. If you can't recall exactly where you got the object or why you kept it in the first place, then it has become clutter. You own a lot of things, and have in the past, and will own more in the future. Everyone's life is a huge cycle of owning and throwing away.

The Biggest Clutter Traps

Beware of the thought, "I might need this some day," or "This might come in handy." If you think this when you pick up an object, then immediately get rid of that object. It is clutter. In fact, most clutter in your house is masquerading as something potentially useful.

When it comes to gifts people have given you, remember the old adage, "It's the thought that counts." If you don't use a gift, and it won't be missed, give it away or throw it out. The caring and thoughtfulness that went into the gift is enough in itself, no matter that the gift is perfect or that it doesn't suit you at all. Don't keep that enormous juicer if you're allergic to citrus or if you already have two others. Don't add to the clutter in your life out of a sense of obligation to the person who has given a gift to you.

Alternatives to Throwing Away Clutter

Aside from the often unworkable practice of regiving gifts, you can often turn unusable gifts or unneeded objects into something useful. A cookie jar can become a nail holder, a vase a penny holder. Use your throwaway clothes as cleaning rags and your old welcome mat as a dog bed. If you like to make candles, use an old pot to melt wax and store it with your craft supplies. But don't keep an old pot on the off chance you will want to make candles sometime in the future.

If you can't bear to throw the object out, lend it to someone else. You get the best of both worlds—you are recycling, yet you're not giving the object up for good. In fact, you'll probably forget that your friend has the object, because you never really needed it.

A final word. Don't become compulsive about eliminating clutter. The goal is to clear up your life enough so that clutter is no longer a problem on which you have to spend time or thought. If you're agonizing over the fact that you've cleared out your closets but your backyard still looks like a junk sale—relax. You've accomplished something wonderful already. Wait until satisfaction seeps into you before pressing on.

2 | *Collectors*

Do newspapers or magazines pile up around your house or office?

Is dusting a major chore in your household?

Does your backyard resemble a junkyard?

Some people are perennial collectors of clutter. This chapter examines a few typical types of clutter collectors and has suggestions for changing collecting habits.

Do You Collect Clutter?

Are you the kind of person who saves all the newspapers and magazines you receive, moving them from your coffee table to under the table and then into the closet? Perhaps you eventually cut or tear out some articles and put them into files, while most of the periodicals lie in piles around the house. When these piles start spilling from beneath your desk and out of every corner, you know you have a problem with Information Collecting.

Many people collect knickknacks...thimbles, plates, owls, unicorns.... You receive them as gifts or buy them yourself. Knickknack collecting can be an interesting and

8

fun way to channel your collecting instincts, but when your shelf of glass-blown figurines grows to four shelves, then into drawers and further on to boxes, you have a problem with Knickknack Collecting.

Then there are those people who will collect anything: objects they find on the street, objects their friends and neighbors are getting rid of, even objects their spouse tries to get rid of. These people don't necessarily go out and buy more objects, but odd bits and pieces seem to gravitate to them. Do you build sheds and install shelves or cabinets to house these things you think will come in handy? The Junk Collecting habit is the most harmful, simply because there is a never-ending source of throw-away objects just waiting to be picked up.

With all of these collecting habits, the most important consideration is your time. If your collecting habit takes up more time than the objects are worth, then your collecting has gotten out of control. Do you spend hours dusting your knickknacks or building your sheds to hold your junk? A little can be a wonderful thing; overabundance is clutter. The key to eliminating useless clutter is to evaluate the items you collect.

Information Collecting

When in doubt, throw resource information away. You can find those same magazines or newspapers in your local library whenever you need them. The articles are cataloged according to subject and author in the library— easy to find and copy.

Don't keep articles simply because you read them and found them interesting. You'll read many interesting articles during your life. If you don't need the information for a certain project you have in mind, then don't keep the article. Besides, most magazines are cyclical in their interests. You'll likely see the same sort of article again in a few years.

If you feel you must keep a record of these articles, write down the name of the periodical and the title of the article and the name of the author. File it where you will need it most. Form an Interesting Articles file if that's the kind of article you keep wanting to save. Note how often you go to this file to refer to the list of articles. It won't be often—just about as often as you read those old periodicals.

Do you have old comics you've been saving for forty years, waiting for a time when they will be valuable? Or when your grandchildren can read them? If you have boxes of periodicals *waiting* for action, then take action. Find out if those magazines are worth anything. Give the comics to your grandchildren. Don't save periodicals when they aren't being regularly read or used by the family.

Information clutterers are lucky. You don't have any decisions to make or sorting to do. All you have to do is dump your piles of periodicals and stacks of clipped articles. Keep reminding yourself that they're a waste of space, they're unsightly, and they're dust collectors. If you persistently save newspapers and magazines, cure yourself of this habit now.

Remember—you can always get hold of this information more quickly and easily than if you let your periodicals pile up into unwieldy stacks.

Knickknack Collecting

When dust clings to every surface because of an overabundance of knickknacks, then it's time to make a change.

Often, certain types of knickknacks become a personal

sign of the collector—you could not imagine living without your collection. To overcome your reluctance to part with a collection, think of the many things that you adored when you were a child. You couldn't imagine giving them up, but you eventually did. You undoubtedly parted with all your old toys because an adult—at some point—helped you decide that you should get rid of them.

Become your own adult! Decide for yourself that you will no longer be burdened with an overabundance of knickknacks spread through your house. Are you afraid that throwing the knickknacks out will cause a severe emotional deprivation? Then wrap them up and store them in a box. All of them.

Get used to the knickknacks being gone from your sight. After a few months, or even a year, go through the box of treasures. You will see how little you missed those knickknacks. Oh, you'll remember them when you see them, but notice how often you exclaim, "I forgot about this one!" or "Now I remember this one!" You forgot you had these knickknacks, yet your life was not deprived in any way.

After storing the knickknacks for some time, try giving them away or selling them. Or simply throw them away. You may choose to keep a few, but the decision will be easier because your feelings will be more defined after not seeing the knickknacks for a while.

Getting rid of your possessions can be hard, even traumatic, at first. You've invested so much of your care and time on those knickknacks and have identified yourself with them for so long. But you are faced with a unique opportunity: to change your life for the better. You can truly become someone new when your old habits and associations are gone. You can look to the future, rather than huddling over your things to reassure you of who you are.

Junk Collecting

You walk a fine line when you salvage junk. Recycling is the wave of the future, and it's good to reuse objects rather than introducing a new item into the world. So if you always need wood, by all means salvage the wood you find. But when your woodpile looms as tall as you are, then it's time to reconsider the wisdom of salvaging wood. You obviously don't use as much wood as you thought. When you begin to salvage on the premise that "I might need this some day," you're on the wrong track.

Beware of these phrases: "I know someone who could use this" and "This is practically new" and "This could come in handy." These imply that the object is not wanted now, but may be wanted in the future. *Always* throw away objects you're saving simply because you might need them in the future—it's a sure sign of clutter. If you have piles of junk that are waiting to be useful, then start throwing things away and stop picking up clutter.

3 | *Household Clutter*

Do you cringe when someone visits your home? Is your living room presentable, but your kitchen a mess?

Do you regularly put things in the first handy place you come to while cleaning your house?

An efficient and well-kept house is an impossible dream, right? Wrong. Only two things need to be considered when you want to bring order to your house: the systems used to organize your possessions, and the way members of your household take responsibility for maintaining order. This chapter will focus on organizational systems for each room of your house.

Except for rare occasions, activities should be confined only to one area of the house. Your exercise equipment shouldn't be in both the living room and the bedroom. Games shouldn't be in both the children's rooms and the den.

Living Room

The living room or den has the most potential for becoming cluttered. Objects naturally gravitate to the living room because it is the center of the household. Don't attempt to keep your family's possessions from the living room; that will simply render it useless.

Do consider whether every activity that goes on in the living room should continue to be done there. Perhaps it would be better if you kept your sewing kit in your bedroom or workroom. Exercise space could also be switched. Hobbies should be confined to one area and provided with adequate storage space. If the living room is often noisy, then put the phone in a different room, such as the foyer, the breakfast nook, or under the stairs.

If your house has both a den and a living room, designate certain activities for each. You could keep one room especially clean for entertaining, while the other retains a more casual atmosphere where snacks and games are permitted.

If children will be playing in your living room, designate an area belonging to them. This is necessary, or you will be faced with the children's clutter spread across the entire room. Designate one corner complete with storage for toys, games, or creative supplies, a table and a chair, perhaps even a television for video games or extra space to set up elaborate "play" with trains or cars. Impress on the children that this is *their* space and that their things belong in this area, not scattered throughout the living room. Or set up a similar area in the children's bedrooms, allowing them only limited playtime in the living room. Expect maximum clutter when children play mainly in the living room and their toys and games are stored in the bedroom.

If your family plays cards or games in the living room, store the decks and games in a handy drawer or on a low shelf in a nearby closet.

The Cleaning-Out Process

Start small. Choose one corner first, or take one unit of furniture at a time (sofa, coffee table, end table). Consider each object, including the furniture, and determine whether it truly belongs in the living room.

Your possessions should be stored near the area where they are used. Old magazines and newspapers should not be piled up in the living room. They should be dealt with according to Chapter 2, "Collectors." But a heating pad may be stored in an end table if you always use it while sitting on the sofa.

Gather similar objects and store them in the same area. Don't fill empty niches with miscellaneous objects, because that translates into clutter. Kept along with the heating pad could be your sewing box (if you sew in the living room), reading glasses, books waiting to be read—whatever else you do while using the heating pad. Coasters, ashtrays, and matches could be in one drawer. TV trays, folding chairs and card table naturally go together. Liquor, glasses, ice bucket, tongs, and corkscrew should be in one cabinet.

Often, one multipurpose wall unit with cabinets and shelves provides the best organizer for your living room. Lacking such a unit, you can use a large sideboard with divided drawers and shelves to store your possessions.

Workroom

The workroom is the best place for multiple activities. With a large work surface, you can set up storage for each hobby or activity. Additional surfaces can be set up for semipermanent activities: building models, jigsaw puzzles, ironing board for sewing, typewriter table, and so on. These tables should be the right height for working, either standing or sitting.

Proper storage for the items used on each work surface should be nearby, either in a drawer or on a shelf. Shelves above or to one side of the work surface serve as excellent active storage. Buy plastic bins or baskets to hold your projects together and to keep them from mixing with supplies for other projects.

A pegboard over the main work area is a good place to hang your supplies and tools. They are visible and within easy reach. If you like, outline the tool or label the peg to remind you where everything goes. You will be able to see more clearly which tools and supplies you use and which are outmoded or unnecessary. Get rid of any items you never use.

Be sure to clean off the main work surface after you are done for the day, especially if you're not certain which project you will be working on next.

Kitchen

To eliminate clutter in the kitchen, store things in the most logical and convenient place. If you put the frequently used items in the handiest places, kitchen clutter will be easy to spot. Store your glasses in the cupboard by the refrigerator, put the coffee mugs on the shelf over the coffee machine, hang the pot holders beside the oven.

Keep Similar Items Together

Keep similar items together on each shelf, but don't necessarily keep all the drinking glasses in one cabinet, all the plates in another, and so on. It is more helpful to store items used together in the same place, such as baking utensils. The rolling pin, mixing bowls, and sifter should all go on the same shelf.

China and service ware of the same pattern needn't be stored together, either. If you have six people in your family, put six of each pattern on a handy shelf. The others can be stored on a less accessible shelf.

Duplicates

Go through each drawer and shelf. If you have unnecessary duplicates, like several can openers or four knife sharpeners, keep only one or, at most, two. Give the others away, or throw them out. If you haven't used your eggbeater in two years, toss it out. When you need one, you can buy another. If you have lots of space, group your utensils in two drawers, those you often use, and those you only use when doing the Christmas baking.

The same can be said of plates, glasses, and pots and pans. Five frying pans and no space for your new pressure cooker? Throw out a few frying pans. Twenty-four shot glasses and no space for your tea glasses? Give most of those shot glasses to a friend who likes to have parties.

Appliances and Accessories

If you use canisters, keep them all in one area. If you don't use canisters, they are clutter and you should get rid of them.

Get rid of that bulky knife block. You can either store your knifes in a drawer organizer or in a handy organizer that attaches to the bottom of one of you cabinets. It folds out of sight and keeps your knives from being jumbled together in a drawer.

A lazy susan can revive a uselessly deep corner cabinet. Put your spices on it, or canisters, or utensil jugs.

Put away all appliances that aren't used daily. If your toaster oven is only used on Sundays, assign it a suitably handy shelf or drawer. The same goes for cookbooks.

Spice racks are good; they limit the amount of space your spices can take up, thereby ensuring you will monitor which are used and which are not. Alphabetize your spices. This will take a small amount of effort, and the result will be an organized rack with every kind of spice easy to find.

A basket is good for holding fruit. It makes a colorful display and puts the fruit where everyone is prompted to eat it.

Your refrigerator is a prime clutter-collector. Organize the shelves and you will eliminate the pockets where food collects. Store frequently served foods on the most accessible space, but remember to group similar foods together. Chose a prominent place for leftovers so that you can see them before they spoil. Date and label all wrapped leftovers that go into the freezer.

Don't leave your ironing board up. If that's a habit you can't break, then invest in an ironing board that attaches to the back of a door in your kitchen or pantry. They are easy to install, and you will always flip the board up when you're done—if only to be able to close the door. No more problem!

Bedroom

The best place to put frequently used items is on a handy shelf (for books or knitting) or on a bedside table with a drawer (for flashlight, pad of paper, pen, extra pair of reading glasses, or cards). A strategically placed table or shelf is also handy if you plan to snack in bed. These surfaces should only be used for frequently used items, not as long- or mid-term storage. Clear anything out of this area if you don't use it at least a couple of times a week.

If you have space for a reading spot on a desk or exercise equipment in your bedroom, define the area and keep in it only those things that pertain to the activity there. If you always undress in one area, designate that as the clothes catchall, rather than letting dirty clothing spread around the room.

Under the bed is a good place for long-term storage, but beware of this habit. As with boxed storage (see Chapter 4, "Storage"), you at least once a year should go through everything you keep under your bed and eliminate anything not used or absolutely needed as a memento.

Because this is a storage place that is more accessible than the back of a closet or the basement or attic, don't store boxed mementos under your bed. Instead, put there the things you will need to get to semiregularly, such as off-season clothing or luggage.

Bathroom

Bathrooms offer limited options for organization. That is why manufactured organizers work best in the bathroom. The shower should have a tray for shampoo, conditioner, razor, shaving cream, and so on. Makeup should be kept in one container or on one shelf.

The bathroom collects clutter faster than any room in the house. Health and beauty aids that are half-used, never used, rarely used, old and crusty, probably fill your bathroom storage space. Eliminate everything that you aren't using anymore. Be ruthless; these aren't possessions that you are getting rid of, but packaged goods that can be bought anywhere, at any time, for little money.

You should assess the storage capacity of your bathroom. Then, according to the number of people who will be using the bathroom, designate areas for each person's private storage. Also designate areas that are for general storage.

Storage should follow the usual rule: Keep items that are similar together. First-aid items, such as Band-Aids, aspirin, and antiseptic, should go on one shelf or in one box clearly marked First Aid and be placed in general storage.

Grooming items, such as deodorant, lotion, and tweezers, should be grouped together in each person's private storage. If you have a large quantity of makeup, sort it into small baskets or boxes and keep it in your private storage. If there is one large makeup box, find an appropriate place for it under the sink or on a larger shelf.

Everything for the shower should be kept in the shower. Towels and washcloths should be kept together under the sink or in a small dresser inside the bathroom so they are handy, rather than in the linen closet. Toilet paper, feminine hygiene products, and paper cups could also be kept under the sink, while the cleansing products should be placed in a container on a shelf or under the sink.

Medicine Cabinet

How many bottles of old pills do you have in your medicine cabinet? How many packages of cold tablets with only three or four pills left in the foil-backed holders? Most people collect medicine unthinkingly, but this can be dangerous. Expiration dates pass, labels wear or crumble off, and assorted pills with no markings lurk in every corner. The least dangerous thing that can happen is a medicine has lost its effectiveness, but that's little comfort when you have a cut or a cold. Or medicine can be mixed up, causing you to take a pill for constipation instead of one for a headache. The worst thing that can happen is the nightmare of medicine cabinet lore—an external medicine ingested or a pet antibiotic taken by people.

An old prescription medication should *always* be thrown away after you have recovered from an illness. Keeping one that is used regularly for a chronic condition (thyroid, hypertension, etc.) is necessary, of course. The point is that antibiotics lose their effectiveness with time, and there is the risk that a doctor will be unable to properly analyze your symptoms if you've already begun self-treatment with leftover medicine.

Over-the-counter medicines also should be thrown out once the expiration date has passed. If you can't find the date or can't decipher it or can't remember specifically when you bought it (but know it was more than six months ago), throw it out. Also dispose of pills, capsules, tablets, you're not sure of. Get rid of those anonymous, mysterious pills now.

Any external medicine over a year old usually should be tossed. Age and air can affect medicine, lessening its effectiveness.

Foyer

The foyer should always be a general-use area and therefore should be kept clear of clutter. It is the first place visitors see, and you want their impression to be favorable.

If objects must be stored in the foyer, be sure to have proper storage for them. The shelf in the closet should hold possessions you often use rather than long-term storage. Outdoor toys and games, binoculars and sporting equipment, should be kept in this closet.

Install low hooks on the back of the door for outdoor

clothing. Hooks are much easier and quicker to get to than hangers. Hats, coats, scarves, and gloves with strings can also be hung up. Or you can string a clothesline with clothespins to hang gloves and mittens. Boots should be stored on a dripping rack on the bottom of a closet nearest the door.

A coatrack is good for older children and adults and especially guests. Make certain the stand is on a hard surface rather than carpet so that dripping rain and snow won't harm it.

You should also have an umbrella stand. You will always have umbrellas, and this is the most convenient way to store them. Buy a conventional stand or a large decorated vase.

Summary of Household Clutter

1. Pick one place for each activity and keep all objects associated with that activity in that area.
2. Start small when clearing clutter from your house. Don't tackle the entire house; start with one area of one room.
3. Store possessions near the place where they are most often used.
4. Gather similar objects together and store them in the same place.
5. Get rid of duplicates or old and worn-out items, especially medicines.

4 | *Household Clutterers*

Do you shudder every time someone comes into your house?

Is your spouse a chronic clutterer?

Do you despair over teaching your children how to keep from cluttering the living room?

People produce clutter. So when you want to eliminate it, you have to see that each person assumes responsibility for it and shares in the task of maintaining order. This chapter therefore focuses on the members of your household and provides helpful hints on how to get everyone involved in eliminating clutter from your lives.

Assigning Responsibilities

If clutter is a common household problem, then you need to call a meeting. Everyone living in your home, whether a roommate, a spouse, a child, or a relative must acknowledge that clutter is a problem. If you have trouble getting them to pay attention and take this problem seriously, insist that everyone admit out loud that the household has a clutter problem. Each person should acknowledge his or her responsibility for trying to make a change.

Agree on a specified length of time, perhaps a week to start with, in which to change. Get your housemates to commit themselves to leaving a room in better shape than when they entered it. That means they'll be restacking the magazines on the coffee table or throwing out magazines they no longer want or taking a used glass into the kitchen or sorting through an old pile of stuff stacked in a corner. They don't have to make a huge effort, because if everyone follows this rule, your house will gradually become clutter-free. The effort will also help you pinpoint the trouble spots where things accumulate.

Spouse

Compromise is in order when one or both partners are clutterers. Usually each person has his or her own special problem—for example, the husband may be a collector while the wife can't organize her time.

First, each must respect the other spouse's right to live as he or she wants to. But it follows as a corollary that neither spouse has the right to inconvenience the other. These two principles must be kept in balance. One person's habits or preferences should not be allowed to disrupt the household or prevent another from living normally.

Each person should have his or her own private space, be it a desk or a room. The private spaces should be as equal as possible; otherwise tensions will arise. If you have one extra room, divide it with bookshelves, put up temporary screens, or build a partition. Hobbies and work should be done in the private space rather than in the general areas. No one should be allowed to consistently clutter the dining room table as well as his or her own desk or room.

Depending on the size of your house, each spouse may have more than one private area. Determine which areas belong to whom, then designate the remainder of the house as general-use areas. The general-use areas should always be cleared of your clutter after you use it, unlike your private area which may be left semicluttered if you are in the middle of a project.

Set a good example, just as you do with your children. With separate private areas, it will become increasingly clear who is organized and who is not.

If you're a housewife and your spouse claims ignorance as justification for clutter—he doesn't know what to do with clothes, paperwork, dishes, or cleaning—then take the time to demonstrate exactly how the task is done or where the objects go. And if you're the husband, don't let your spouse consistently walk away without learning where the tools she uses should go. The house, the possessions, belong to both of you, and you both should know how to take care of them.

Cleaning

Set aside one day or a couple of evenings each week when both partners will do general cleaning. You can either rotate chores or do the same tasks every week. This schedule needn't be rigid: if one person has to miss the cleaning night, the chores can wait until the next day.

For daily tasks, each should have set tasks. Sit down and talk it out. Perhaps you hate to do the dishes but don't mind making the bed and straightening the bedroom.

Both spouses should be conscientious in performing their tasks. Men, even today, still do less than ten minutes of housework a week while women generally do eighty minutes. Try to change these statistics in your own home.

If nothing works, then stop picking up after your spouse. Let the laundered clothes lie in piles around the bedroom; let the dishes lie in the sink. Point out what you are doing and explain exactly why you are doing it. Unless you are being paid by your spouse to be a maid or butler, then you don't have to do their cleaning for them.

Children

You don't want to nag or pick up after your children, so what are the alternatives? Children can be taught organizational skills, and the younger they start, the better prepared they will be for the rest of their lives.

Make putting things away as easy as possible. An adjustable tension rod is a handy way to make hanging clothes easy for children's reach. It can be adjusted as the children get older. The hamper should stay in the closet or bedroom, not the bathroom.

Toy Storage

If your children always play in the basement, put the toy storage there, even if the basement is used as a family den. An attractive wooden box is a better alternative to having stuffed animals and action dolls scattered across the floor. If your children routinely throw their toys (or clothes for that matter) in a particular area, put the toy box or hamper there. Then you don't have to fight their old habits completely to get them to clean up their clutter.

If the majority of your children's play will take place in the bedroom, arrange a corner for toy and game storage, as well as creative supplies.

Buy a table and chair that are comfortable for the children. They should be allowed to keep special projects out on their table or in a particular corner of the room (to set up a doll house or race track), but the rest of the floor and the bed should be cleared of clutter each day, and the toys and games should be put in their proper places.

A single large storage box is not necessarily the best alternative—the toys become jumbled and difficult to find. Low shelves, stackable bins, drawers or several boxes are good ways to organize toys. Small toys and games should be kept in boxes, bins, or baskets so that they aren't loose in larger containers. Mark the outside of the bins or containers with a picture of the toy or a colored label (if the child is old enough to read) so that the contents are clear.

When your child gets a new game or toy, help decide where its storage place will be. Don't make children's decisions for them, as that will ensure they won't learn how to do it for themselves. Besides, it is their room and children should have a say in where their possessions go.

Cleaning

When it is time to clean up the room, prompt your child to see the scattered toys and clothing as objects that have their proper places. Ask them to fetch all the big toys or stuffed animals first and put them in their place. Then gather the smaller toys together. Then the creative supplies. Then the clothes. This categorizes the objects in the child's mind rather than forcing him or her to do the more daunting task of working systematically from door to bed.

Set clear standards for cleaning. Does the blanket have to be folded every day, or the sheets smoothed and tucked? Can the toy cars be put with the soldiers? Can all the craft supplies be jumbled together in one box?

Keep the cleaning tasks suited to the child's age. When a child is very young, you should help in the cleaning. While the child picks up the blocks, you gather the stuffed animals. As the child gets older, his or her responsibilities should increase.

Make a game of the cleaning, or tell a story while you work. This will create good associations in the child's mind with clearing clutter from his or her room.

The best way to teach your child how to keep clutter from invading the household is by example. Both parents should help keep the house clean, and they should include the children as much as possible in the process.

Getting Rid of Children's Clutter

Helping a child learn when it is time to get rid of unused or old possessions prevents another clutter-collector from joining the population. Approach clutter elimination with the attitude that "things" are in a constant motion. Possessions come into your life, and at some point they leave it.

If a child resists throwing or giving something away, never force it. Explain your own system of putting objects aside that you aren't sure of so that you can decide over time whether you want to keep that possession. Have a "think-about-it" area—a shelf or space set aside in the child's room for these objects where he or she can see them. Let the child decide whether to keep the object or get rid of it.

Children are allowed to be pack rats more than adults because their possessions become invested with meaning that parents may not know about or understand. Don't create a lifetime pack rat by being too compulsive about your child throwing away his or her belongings. As children grow up, they will naturally discard things they are "too old" to play with.

If there are many toys and games that aren't often played with, store them for a few months, then bring them out again. It will add novelty to them, and if the child still doesn't play with them, then it's time to suggest getting rid of these toys. If the child hesitates, put the toy in the think-about-it area.

Adolescents

By the time your children grow into adolescence, hopefully you will have instilled proper clutter-consciousness in them so that you don't have to battle over messy rooms. If an adolescent perennially keeps a cluttered room, then the cause may be something other than a lack of organization or cleanliness.

Adolescents don't want to be told what to do about themselves or their possessions. Further complicating this, their privacy is of utmost importance. If you can deal with it, simply tell your children to keep their doors closed until they outgrow their messiness.

It's not a good idea to clean the rooms of adolescents for them. They will never be faced with the results of their lack of effort if you do it for them. Besides, most adolescents don't want their parents in their rooms, or drawers, or closets, and parents should respect that right. It's part of growing up and moving out from under the protective parental umbrella.

5 | *Storage*

*Do you toss objects in the first handy place when you
want them out of sight?*

Do odds and ends lurk in every corner?

Is your linen closet beside your kitchen?

Most of your possessions are stored in some manner
until it is time to use them. This chapter deals with the
basics of clearing out and organizing shelves, closets,
drawers, and other storage areas.

Where

When deciding where an object should be kept, remember two important questions. The answers will
provide rules for storage.

1. How often is the object used? Store it high or conveniently low accordingly.
2. Where is the object used? Store it in a place convenient
   to its use.

The more frequently you use an object, the more
accessible it should be. Ideally, all frequently used objects

should be stored in the handiest areas—on reachable shelves, in cabinets, and in drawers.

Objects that aren't used as often (small things like maps, reference books, candles, and magnifying glass) should have their own storage places as well. But these don't have to be as easily accessible as the small, frequently used items.

Larger items that you use less often—your sewing machine, typewriter, electric blanket, and fan—should be stored safely, but not necessarily at your fingertips. Try to keep these things together in one out-of-the-way place. You'll find yourself automatically turning to that place when you think of a useful object you don't use often. If you scatter these possessions among your active objects, they start to look like clutter.

At some point, you'll find yourself surrounded by objects that have no clearly defined category and no relation to other miscellaneous objects. Don't simply store them in the first handy space; it will defeat your purpose of organization. You will never remember where everything is.

Consider the use of the object. Binoculars are generally used outside the house. So a closet or shelf near the door most frequently used is the best location. If you vacuum your living room more often than your bedroom, put the vacuum in the closet nearest to the living room rather than in the garage. If you exercise in the den, then store the equipment there.

Keep similar objects together. Put all office supplies in one drawer, all underwear in another. Sounds fairly simple, doesn't it? Well, what about your junk drawer? The one that holds various bits of often-used stuff—from office supplies to champagne corks, from matches to hair ribbons. That's clutter.

Odds and Ends

Small stuff that tends to slide under the sofa cushions, objects that fill junk drawers because there's no other place for them, keys, matches, candles, flashlights, loose change—these things belong in storage containers or racks.

Have a certain drawer or shelf for these objects, with individual containers for each type. Then, if you come across a small piece of clutter, you can return it to its proper place.

Matches, candles, and flashlights should be stored together in the same drawer. Of course, it's good to have several small storage places for these items in case of a power outage. Put a few candles and matches in a handy box in the hall closet, in a small drawer in the kitchen, and in your bedside table.

Loose change should be collected in one place. If you accumulate a lot of change, have separate containers for each kind. Store the loose change in the place where you most often pull it out of your pocket or purse. If it's when you take off your clothes at night, collect the change in your bathroom or bedroom. If it's when you clean out your purse, put a basket or dish in your office area. If it's after grocery shopping, put a jar in the kitchen.

Keys should always be marked for their use: back door, front door, shed, country house, gate, etc. Padlocks not in use should always have their key in the lock. Most keys should be hung. If you put them in a basket, the useless keys can linger for the rest of your life, especially if they aren't marked.

A key holder with each hook marked is the best alternative to a basket or jar. The holder should be placed beside a door for easy access and low enough for responsible children to reach.

If you always come in the front door, but the other keys are stored at the back door, put a hook or basket by the front door for your car and house keys. This will eliminate the constant problem of misplacing your keys.

Things people usually think are odds and ends should often be stored with other similar objects. Shoe polish, sunglasses, and lint brush are clothing accessories. Coasters and ashtrays should be stored in the same place as your place mats and tablecloths, or in a drawer in the living room where they will be used. Scratch paper should be stored in several places, such as by phones and near doors for messages. Safety pins are bathroom accessories, as are Band-Aids, hair ties, and sunscreen. Small toys should be kept in a box with larger toys, not scattered throughout the house.

Closets

Make certain that each closet best suits your needs. What will you be storing in the closet? Books, games, linen, supplies? Does the closet have shelves? Are they spaced to make maximum use of the closet? Is the closet in a useful area of the house for its storage purpose?

If you're storing children's games, they should be handy to the child so you won't have to remove them. If it's linen, the closet should be near the laundry. The pantry should be next to the kitchen. Assess your house and, if necessary, reassign closets to better suit your needs. A closet between the living room and kitchen that is currently filled with photographic equipment, albums, assorted boxes or luggage, could be reassigned to hold kitchen overflow, such as spare china, tablecloths, and TV trays.

How you store your possessions depends on how often

you use them. Clear plastic bins should be used for objects you need to get to regularly. Jars and open baskets are another alternative. These storage containers should be kept on the most handy shelves.

When storing your possessions for a long time, boxes are most convenient. Be sure to label the box clearly on several sides. Record its number and what it contains on a piece of paper to keep in your files.

Go through your boxes from time to time (moving is a particularly good time) and throw out what is no longer useful or a definite memento. Still, once your clutter is boxed, on the assumption that you have plenty of storage, you don't have to be as ruthless in throwing things away. You've already moved it from the clutter category to the storage category. Ask yourself if you are keeping these items on the chance that they will someday be useful. If you are, that's when you throw them out.

If there's no light in the closet, store a flashlight on one of the handy shelves. Or you can sink a hook in the ceiling and attach the flashlight to a long string. You can tie a slipknot to dangle the flashlight over your head for illumination, or leave the string free so that you can hold the flashlight in your hand to search corners.

Cleaning Out Closets

Choose one closet to start on and decide on its best use. Have boxes handy for throwaway and boxes marked for storage in other closets.

If you've decided that the hall closet will hold general family storage, such as tools, equipment, photo albums, and games, you can begin organizing that closet, removing all kitchen, bedroom, and clothing storage.

When reorganizing a closet, don't pull everything out at once and pile it around you. Work on one shelf at a time.

Pick up each object and ask yourself if you've used this in the past year. The past two years? Ever? What are you holding onto it for? Does it have sentimental meaning for you?

If you can't pinpoint the usefulness or your attachment to the object, ask yourself if it might come in handy someday. If the answer is yes, get rid of it—throw the object out or give it away. It's clutter if it doesn't have a purpose right now in your life. Refer to Chapter 1, "How to Eliminate Clutter," if you need to again assure yourself that you can let go of your possessions.

Redistribute objects to their proper places. Papers should go in the office area, books in the bookshelves, clothes in your clothes closet. It might help to have several boxes as catchalls, to semisort the objects you pull from the closet until they can be stored in their proper place.

Put the object aside if it should return to the closet you are working on, or put it in the appropriate box. Once you've cleared the unused and out-of-place items, you can begin arranging the closet you are working on.

Frequently used items should be stored on low and middle shelves, and less-used ones on top shelves and in the back. Keep items used at the same time together—such as bowling ball, bag, and shoes or projector and slides. Never stack more than three items on top of one another.

Creating New Storage Space

Often a clutter problem is really a space problem. You don't have room for everything, so it becomes jumbled together and everything becomes difficult to find. Then you can't use your possessions as you would like to because they are not easy to access.

Always organize existing space before trying to add new furniture or shelves. Never buy a new filing cabinet or dresser or install new shelves until you've gone through everything in the old storage space and thrown out as much as you can. If you don't do that, eventually you'll have rooms of concealed clutter.

If you simply don't have room, then it's time to add space.

A warning: Keep an eye out for small spaces, such as the area next to your couch, or a bare wall in your bathroom. Whatever you do, don't fill every niche. The beauty of getting rid of clutter is discovering and cherishing those small spaces. Think of them as the frames in your house, setting off a group of furniture or balancing a room. When searching for new space, always keep the frames in mind.

Think creatively. You don't want to get out the electric screwdriver until it's absolutely necessary. Shelves can be used to store items other than books. With small clutter, it's best to place the items in baskets or boxes so that the shelf still looks attractive. Or you can hang an interesting drape over the lower shelves to hide the storage behind it. With larger objects, such as typewriters, fans, and sleeping bags, store these on the bottom and top shelves of large bookcases.

Toy boxes can be also used as general game holders for adults. Or your antique hope chest can be filled with linen or stored clothing. If your files only fill one drawer in your cabinet, then use the other to store supplies.

Use screens and curtained corners and niches to hide loaded shelves or a full area of your house. This way you turn an eyesore into a decorative asset. In a similar way, you place tall bookcases so that they jut into the room, creating a niche in a large room. A desk or table can be placed inside this new alcove for added privacy. This is particularly useful for wide bookcases which allow for storage from both sides.

Objects designed for organizing your clutter usually don't work as well as you'd like. But in a few essential areas, you can get a lot of use out of them. For the shower; a container to hold soap, shampoo, conditioner, shaving cream, razor, etc. Utilize a sewing box or travel kits for makeup or hair articles. Small and large containers and racks to organize your odds and ends are almost essential.

Shelves

The best place to build shelves is in a closet. Then you don't have to worry about having unsightly items in plain view. In large closets, line one side with shelves. This is especially good for children. One side of the closet can be used for clothes and the other for toys.

In shallow closets, there is the danger of the shelves being too deep if you shelve in the entire space. Perhaps the bottom shelf could be the width of the closet, but the others should be narrower. Otherwise, your possessions will disappear into the dark recesses, never to be seen again. Always remember, you're building shelves to make things handy, not hide them away.

If you don't want to go to the trouble of building shelves, simply place a large chest of drawers in the closet. This doesn't use all the available space, but it is an easy solution.

In small rooms, especially the pantry or laundry or furnace rooms, build shelves supported by floor-to-ceiling posts. This dramatically increases the use of those rooms which were intended to store quantities of objects.

If possible, install adjustable shelves. Then store items of the same height on the same shelves. You can also add more shelves later if needed.

In bedrooms, a shelf just below the ceiling all around

the room is a decorative way to store items not used frequently. In children's rooms, stuffed animals, dolls or figurines may be displayed as well as books, photo albums or mementos you wish to keep on display rather than store in boxes. A good way to retrieve these items is by using an expandable pincher claw. Everyone should have a tool such as this, or a similar one, to retrieve small items fallen behind or under heavy furniture.

Plants either may be hung or shelved. Try to keep plants off the top of tables. Good places for shelves may be a corner near a window, within the window frame itself, or under the window. Plants can also be hung from a ceiling hook with a butterfly bolt, or from a triangle hinge attached to the wall.

Hanging Items

Hooks placed on the backs of doors provide the most convenient method of hanging. You use space that is currently going to waste while keeping the hanging objects out of sight. Nightgowns, pajamas, and bathrobes can be hung on the back of the bathroom door, outdoor clothing on the back of a hall closet near the door, shoes in a hanging shoe tree, or ties on multiple hangers hung on a hook on the back of your closet door. Be inventive. Anything that you often use is a good candidate for hanging on the back of a door.

If you don't have enough door space, place hooks along the back of the closet for your camera, binoculars, extra purses, and bags. Anything with a shoulder strap can be hung as storage.

If your space is very limited, consider hanging possessions from the ceiling or high on the wall. These can include exercise equipment, bicycles, folding chairs, TV trays, musical instruments, etc. Large pegs will serve to remove these objects from your way while making them easy to reach.

New Possessions

When you buy a new possession for the house, decide immediately where its permanent storage place will be. Don't assume it will fall into the right place automatically; that will ensure that the item sits around indefinitely until you get tired of looking at it.

When you decide right away, you might eventually have to move it to a new place that's more convenient, but at least the new possession never becomes clutter. This will also keep you from acquiring useless objects if you know you will have to find a place for them as soon as you return home.

Summary of Storage

1. How often is the object used? Store it high or conveniently low accordingly.
2. Where is the object used? Store it in a place convenient to its use.
3. Keep similar objects together.
4. Always organize existing space before trying to add new furniture or shelves.
5. Look to shelves and hooks as the best storage options.
6. Always decide where a new possession will be stored as soon as you bring it into the house.

6 | *Clothing Clutter*

Have you ever found an article of clothing that you forgot you had?

Are your belts and scarves jumbled together on the floor of your closet?

Do you have fourteen skirts and only two shirts?

Even if you spend thousands of dollars, your attempts to assemble a complete wardrobe can be easily destroyed if your useful clothes get lost in the clutter. This chapter deals with clothing and accessories—how to sort and store them, when to get rid of them, and when to buy them new.

Sorting

To sort, you must determine whether an item of clothing is: (1) useful, and should be hung up or put in a drawer, (2) useless, and should be thrown away, (3) undecided, and should be put on hold for a year, or (4) a memento, and should be properly stored.

Examining and evaluating your clothes once a year is the best way to organize your wardrobe. Each year, you'll have the benefit of last year's efforts to build on. Eventually, it will become second nature to decide what should happen with each item of clothing, thereby eliminating the clutter.

To examine your clothes, try on everything you haven't worn in the past year. You'll be amazed at the finds you come across. It's like a whole new wardrobe.

. Many people with seasonal wardrobes and small closets store their out-of-season clothes in boxes or seldom-used suitcases. The yearly examination can be done in the spring or fall when it's time to shift your wardrobe from boxes to closets anyway.

Useless Clothing

The easy choices are the clothes you put on and wonder what ever made you to buy a rag like that. Bag those clothes up and take them to the thrift store, or turn them into rags, or have a garage sale, or give them to a friend, or donate them to charity. If your rejected clothes hang around in a bag at the bottom of your closet for another year, then give it up. Recycling is always best, but if you just can't bring yourself to do it, then throw the clothes out.

Undecided Clothing

If you're not sure you like the item of clothing, put it in a special section where you can see it when you open your closet. Then the option is always in front of your eyes. If a year rolls around, and you still haven't worn that skirt or shirt or whatever, you can push it aside.

After another year, if a piece of clothing is still hanging in your closet and you haven't managed to put it on your body except during your yearly checks, then the clothing should be thrown out or stored as a memento.

Mementos

Evaluate the importance of each item of clothing. Does it remind you of a particular event or a time in your life? If you have a whole rack of clothes like this, be ruthless. Pick out your favorites, and hold on to only the unique clothing. Keep only one of the pairs of pants that prove you once fit into a size six—if you absolutely must. After all, it's not the clothes that are important, but your memories of that special trip or the prom.

These treasured pieces should be kept in a separate place. After all, you aren't wearing them anymore, so they don't belong among the other clothes you do wear. They now fall into the category of mementos. If you have adequate storage space, box these clothes up and label the outside clearly on all four sides and the top. If you live where space is limited, you can store your "clothes treasures" in a seldom-used suitcase. That way, a suitcase that's taking up space now has a legitimate purpose in your life.

If a year or two has gone by and you have new items you must add to the memento box, bring the box or suitcase down and get ready for a ride down memory lane. If you pull out several items that remind you of the same thing, person or place, then get rid of two and keep only one. If you can't remember where you wore it, but always liked it, then get rid of it. That's right. You have plenty of things that you like to wear, that you actually wear.

Try to cut down on the bulk of your mementos, but this is where you can restrain yourself for a year or two. If you're not sure, tag an item to remind yourself about it the next time you go through the box. By then, you'll probably be a little more certain you want to get rid of it. If you're not completely certain, tag it again. The next time you look through the box, if the item doesn't make you tingle with memories, get rid of it. It's already

halfheartedly served you for a long time. Don't drag out
the death.

Clothes Closet

What should really be in your clothes closet? Always
keep in mind that this closet is for your clothes. That
thought will keep other types of possessions from accumulating. Your clothing, shoes, and accessories should
get first priority, then boxed clothing and suitcases can be
fit in as long as there's room.

The quickest way to gather useless clothes (or clutter) is
by not knowing what you have. Organizing your closet
will make your wardrobe needs clear at a glance.

Hang as many clothes as possible. With the clothes in
orderly rows, mixing and matching is much easier. In
organizing drawers, put the most frequently used items
in the handiest places. Underwear and nightwear should
be in a prime spot. Sweaters, which are worn only part of
the year, can be put in an out-of-the-way drawer in
summer, then switched with the T-shirts in winter, to
make the sweaters more handy.

Work clothes, play clothes, and dressy clothes should
never be mixed together. Arrange clothing so that the
same types are hung together: shirts with shirts, next to
the jackets, next to the sweaters, and so on. Even if you
have several favorite outfits, don't mix the skirts and
shirts together in the prime space. You're cheating yourself of all the possibilities your wardrobe offers.

Don't keep clothes that are a smaller or larger size
hanging in your closet when you're waiting to diet into or
have just dieted out of them. If seeing these clothes helps
you to diet, then display them prominently, but not
forever. After a while, your eyes will skim over those
jeans and they will no longer give you the benefit of their

impact. The same sorting procedure still applies: make the item handy, and if you haven't worn it in a year, then it's time to remove it from the active lines.

Hang clothes that need to be mended in a special place in your closet. Storing these clothes in drawers is not a good idea, because that puts the items out of sight (therefore out of mind). If the clothes are in front of your eyes, and you know you can't wear them, the incentive to mend them will be greater.

If you're like most people, you take off your clothes at night and toss them somewhere. If you've been doing this all your life, don't expect to be able to mend this habit quickly. *Pick one place* as your toss pile. It can be one chair in your room or the top of the laundry hamper. This is the pile that is waiting to be sorted—things that aren't dirty should be hung up inside out so you'll remember it's already been worn once. The dirty clothes then go into the hamper or laundry bag.

Accessories

Accessories should be organized into a space where they are visible. If you have extra drawers, divide one into compartments or lay the belts and scarves flat, like a fan of cards, so that the edges of all the items are visible.

If you have shelf space, put the accessories in open-ended boxes so you can see what you have. You could also put accessories in shoe trees or hang them from a multiple hanger. If you can see what you have, you can see what you don't use. That's the first step in getting rid of clutter—knowing what you don't use.

Small accessories should have their own "toss place" on a certain area of your dresser or a small table in your bathroom. You must keep in mind, however, that this space is a place of transition. Accessories don't belong permanently in the "toss place," so you have to clean it off every once in a while and put jewelry and hair ribbons back where they belong.

Shoes

You should follow the same yearly examination and sorting procedure with your shoes. Try every pair on at least once a year. Put the maybe's in a prominent place, within easy reach. If you still don't wear those shoes, then it's time to get rid of them.

If they have special meaning to you—your first pair of running shoes, or the shoes you wore at your wedding—then they belong in the memento box. You could store these shoes with your memento clothes. If you're like most people, you won't have too many special "just for the memories" shoes. You could also store these shoes in the most inaccessible pockets of your shoe tree.

Buy a shoe tree. It keeps your active shoes from forming a clutterlike pile on the bottom of your closet. It also keeps your shoes in good shape and displays them for easy access. Most shoe trees hang on the inside of your closet door, so they don't take up needed room. Others are stacks of boxes that can hang from your tension rod.

Buying Clothes

A good way to eliminate clutter from your wardrobe is to plot out what you have and what you need before you go shopping. Otherwise, you'll buy things aimlessly, without a plan in mind, and that leads to clutter.

Take a serious look through your wardrobe. Identify the staples of your casual and work wear. Keep these clothes in mind when you go shopping. Don't duplicate them—that's clutter—but try to buy items that will go with your staples.

Coordination is the key to success with your wardrobe. If you wear browns and beiges, don't buy a shocking pink shirt—no matter how much you're attracted to the bright color. The shirt will lose its appeal and become clutter in your closet. Remember all those fluorescent clothes? How often do you wear them now?

Summary of Clothing Clutter

1. Sort through your clothing and accessories at least once a year, trying everything on and deciding whether it is useful, useless, or undecided or should be stored as a memento.
2. Don't let undecided clothing remain in your closet over a couple years. If you don't wear it, remove it from your closet.
3. Remember that memento clothing should be special, not just an item of clothing you used to like but never wear now.
4. Store similar clothing together—work and play in separate parts of your closet and drawers. Then hang pants with pants and shirts with shirts.
5. Know your wardrobe, and keep in mind colors and needs when shopping. Resist impulse buying.

7 | *Books, Records, and Video Clutter*

Have you ever wanted to read a book you know you own, but couldn't find it in your library?

Does it take you longer than a few minutes to find a book you want?

Do you have stacks of records or cassettes you never listen to?

Your bookshelves don't have to be cluttered. Books, records, and videotapes are easy to organize, and once you've created a system, you won't have to deal with the problem again. This chapter will focus on the techniques necessary to organizing books, records, cassettes, and videotapes.

Books

Most people don't think of clutter in their bookshelves, but it's there. Organizing your library can be a big task. Don't rush and don't worry if you have to leave boxes or piles of books around your house for a few days. The end result will be worth it.

Different techniques apply to sorting books than those

used with typical clutter. You don't necessarily throw away a book that you haven't looked at in one or two years. Instead, your bookshelves should be organized so that you don't lose sight of the fine options you have in your library.

Don't organize each bookshelf separately. Look at all of your books before you begin. If some are boxed and waiting to be shelved, open the box and go through it to see what you have.

You will have to form categories for your library, depending on the types of books you own, and you'll want to make sure you have enough shelf space for each category before shelving the books.

Common categories are:

Art	History
Biography	How-to
Business	Metaphysical
Child Care	Psychological
Cookbooks	Religious
Fiction	Self-help
Gardening	Sports
Health	Travel

You should keep all reference books in one place for *easy* access. Reference books include dictionaries, encyclopedias, atlases, thesauruses, books of quotations, directories, almanacs, and so on.

Within the larger categories, smaller ones may be made. If you own a large number of art books, separate them into groups by artist, period, or country. If you mostly own biographical books, separate them into autobiography and biography, then put them in alphabetical order by last name of the subjects.

Fiction has many categories within it, such as:

Classics	Mystery
Contemporary	Romance
Fantasy	Science Fiction

You may also include poetry, plays, and short stories in your fiction category.

Shelving Books

You can either remove all books from the shelves (and clean the shelves at the same time) or shuffle as you go along. Block out areas for each category before you start, but remember to be flexible. It's difficult to tell how much space you'll need at first.

Books should be shelved according to their category. Choose where each category should go on your shelves. This depends on the frequency of use and the size of each category.

Frequency of use should be the first consideration when shelving books. The largest category of books is not necessarily the one you use the most. If you received your degree in economics, then you may have many business books that you no longer refer to.

After you have decided which categories should be most handy, those which are similar should be grouped together rather than simply arranged alphabetically. Therefore, health should be near self-help; metaphysics, psychology, and religion should be near each other; biography should be near history; while sports, gardening and how-to can be near one another. Art and travel books are often oversized and should be shelved near each other on large enough shelves.

Don't feel like you have to keep your books all in the same place. If you use your many cookbooks, put a shelf in the kitchen or pantry for easy access. Books on car maintenance and repair can go on a shelf in the garage. Most frequently read books can be put on a shelf beside your bed.

Reference books should be the most easily accessible to all members of your family. You may also want an extra dictionary and thesaurus beside your desk.

Make certain you don't cram books into the shelves; leave plenty of space in each category for new books that you acquire. If you own more than one book by an author, you'll probably want to keep those books together when shelving them.

Don't stack books on their sides; that makes removal difficult. You can double layer your books if you have no more space, but be sure to put less-used books in the rear and rotate them every once in a while so that you still have access to them.

Getting Rid of Books

If you don't care enough about a book to want it on a shelf, then consider whether you want to keep it at all. Is it a children's book that you no longer read? If you aren't saving such books for your own children, give them away. Donate them to a library. Some people chose to display these books rather than box them—what you read as a child is often as important as what you read as an adult.

If you received a book as a gift and you have never read it and you probably never will, get rid of it. Often it happens that gift books are not exactly what the recipient likes to read. Don't keep unwanted books around to clutter your shelves.

If you tried to read a book, but put it aside because you hated it, or you bought a book and never got around to reading it, don't throw it away yet. Keep such books together in a special section where you can get to them. These uncertain books should be looked over every once in a while to see if you would like to try to read them now. If a book sits in this section for a few years, it's time to get rid of it.

Don't toss books in the trash. Recycle them along with old newspapers, or give them to friends. Better yet, donated books can become a tax deduction, so if you give them to a school or hospital, keep a record and get a receipt.

New Shelf Space

If you need more space, here are a few options:

- Freestanding bookcases
- Plain wooden cubes that are stackable
- Rows of shelves built into a wall or room divider
- Single shelf where appropriate

Bookcases can be stacked on top of one another (bolted together or to the wall for safety). This makes maximum use of space. Or deep bookcases can be positioned so that both sides of the shelves are accessible.

Records and Cassettes

You will have to form categories for your music library, depending on the types of music you own. Some typical categories include:

Ballads	Jazz
Classical	New Age
Country	Show tunes
Folk	Soft and hard rock

Records and cassettes that consist of spoken words can be categorized into:

Actors or Plays	Lectures
Books on tape	Poetry
Interviews	Self-help

Again, if you have a large category, break it into smaller sections. Classical music can be separated into opera, orchestral, soloists, and chamber music. New Age can be split into instrumental and nature sounds.

Storing Records and Cassettes

Records can be filed in deep bookcases or cubes which have an opening in the front or placed in sturdy cartons which allow access from the top. Cassette tapes are best stored in a cassette carrying case. If your tape collection is large, manufactured cassette containers that can be stacked or hung on the wall are your best option.

Frequency of use should be the first consideration when shelving records or cassettes. The largest category of music is not necessarily the one you listen to the most. Before reorganizing your music library, think carefully about what you listen to. Those categories of music should be the most accessible.

Within the large categories, records and cassettes by the same composer, musician, or performer should always be kept together, forming a subcategory. The subcategories should be arranged alphabetically. Within each, the records and cassettes can either be arranged according to date of release or alphabetically by title.

Beatles records, for example, would form one subcategory within your rock category. If you arrange the records or cassettes according to release date, *Meet the Beatles* would be first, but if you arrange the records alphabetically, then *Abbey Road* would be first.

Mozart records would form one subcategory in your classical category. Depending on the size of your Mozart collection, the records could be arranged according to date of composition or be divided into smaller subcategories—operas, symphonies, soloist, chamber music—which then can be arranged alphabetically, numerically, or by date.

Getting Rid of Records and Cassettes

If you no longer listen to certain records or cassettes, then you should consider whether you want to keep them. Were they records you bought when you were a teenager and are no longer interested in? Keep the records if you occasionally pull them out to travel down memory lane. Music is an important aid to memory, so if you hesitate strongly over a record or cassette, then don't get rid of it.

If you received the music as a gift, and you never have listened to the record and never will, get rid of it. If you bought a record that you don't like, and have tried to listen to it without success, then get rid of it.

Don't toss records or cassettes in the trash. Cassettes can be rerecorded. If you (or a friend) have the machinery to record tape to tape, or album to tape, then keep all your old cassettes. A small piece of tape over the protect hole allows you to copy a whole new album that a friend has lent you, thereby saving yourself the cost of a new cassette.

If you plan on reusing old cassettes, have a special place where you can get to them quickly and where you won't be tempted to try to refile them.

If you do get rid of records and cassettes, give them to a school, hospital, or thrift shop. Like books, these become tax deductions. Keep a record and get a receipt.

Videotapes

Videotapes can be categorized into:

Comedy   Home videos
Documentary   Movies
Exercise   Self-help

Larger categories can be divided into subcategories. Movies are likely to be your largest category. The movies subcategory can include: black and white, classics, humor, romance, adventure, etc. Or you can subcategorize the movies by director or by actor or actress (Bette Davis, The Marx Brothers, Steven Spielberg).

Home videos can be arranged by date or by subject. All Christmas tapes can be kept together, just as all vacation tapes can be kept together. Or simply arrange the videos according to date of taping.

Depending on the number you own, videotapes can be stored on shelves or in tape boxes with sliding drawers.

Getting Rid of Videotapes

If you no longer watch certain movies or no longer use most of your exercise tapes because you prefer one particular one, then it's time to recycle the tape.

Never throw out videotapes you no longer want. Give the movie or self-help tape away, or rerecord over the old material. Cover the protect hole with a piece of tape, and you have a new videotape ready for taping.

Keep the reusable videotapes handy for taping, and don't let them get refiled with your regular tapes.

Never get rid of home videos. You'll almost always regret it if you do.

Summary of Books, Records, and Video Clutter

1. Form categories to organize your books, records, cassettes and videotapes.
2. Break large categories down into subcategories.
3. Arrange the categories according to frequency of use.
4. Store similar categories near one another for ease of accessing.
5. Recycle unwanted books, records, cassettes, and video tapes by giving them to a friend or donating them to charity. Reuse cassettes and videotapes by covering the protect hole and recording over the old information.

8 | *Special Household Problems*

Do you come unglued at the thought of moving?

Do you live in a tiny apartment with little or no storage?

Have you ever thrown out bags and bags of clutter and wished you didn't have to?

Most special household clutter problems are easy to solve by applying rules you've learned throughout this book. This chapter will offer tips on moving, having garage sales, and living in a small apartment.

Moving

Moving into a new home is the best time for removing clutter from your life and organizing systems to keep clutter from accumulating again. You will have to handle every object you own anyway, so this is a good time to implement changes and get rid of clutter.

Make decisions as you pack as to whether you use the object or not, if it belongs in the memento category, whether it could be stored better with similar objects to increase use, or if it should be gotten rid of.

Categories

Just as you store similar objects together, you should pack your household according to certain categories. This will enable you to see exactly what you have. Duplicates and unnecessary and worn-out objects will be easier to distinguish if similar objects are kept together.

Examples of categories are:

- Clothing and accessories
- Children's belongings—toys, games
- Books, records, cassettes, and video tapes
- Kitchen accessories—china, silverware, pots, pans
- Household appliances—toaster oven, clock radio, mixer, microwave
- Household supplies—bug spray, cleaner, rags
- Bathroom accessories—blow drier, toiletries, medicines, plunger and brush
- Linen and towels
- Car accessories
- Office—files, supplies, equipment
- Equipment—exercise, tools, bicycles, lawn mower, typewriter, projector, stereo
- Mementos
- Camping supplies
- Small odds and ends with their storage containers
- Miscellaneous objects—ice bucket, photo albums, luggage, Christmas decorations

Pack and plan to store your possessions within these categories. Examine the floor plans for you new house and decide where everything will go before you move in. Label each box with the intended room as well as its contents, making your unpacking job much easier.

As you pack, don't put objects coming from the same place in the same box. This is the time to sort. Have at least one box for each category open and ready to receive objects at all times. This will prevent "niche filling" in inappropriate boxes.

Have a throwaway and a giveaway box present also. It's psychologically easier to get rid of clutter at this time because *every* object is going into a box. The only thing that is different is the label.

When packing books and records, follow the rules in Chapter 7, "Books, Records, Cassettes, and Videotapes." When you reach your new home, all you have to do is unpack the categories of books onto their new shelves. This is the optimum time to arrange your library and extra bookshelves in the most convenient places.

Since moving is often traumatic for children, don't make them get rid of any of their possessions unless it is absolutely necessary. If they see you disposing of a large amount of clutter, they want to join in. Gently dissuade them. Ask them to help you decide what household items to discard instead. Tell the children you will help them sort through their possessions after the move. Don't try to teach children to get rid of clutter while they are being forced to give up friends and a familiar environment.

Garage Sales

Any time you accumulate a lot of disposable clutter (especially when you move), you should have a garage sale. Literally thousands of dollars can be made from your old junk—and that does mean *junk*. Usually the things you are embarrassed to put out for sale are the ones to go first.

What can you sell? Anything. Clothes, dishes, sports equipment, books, appliances, furniture, knickknacks, etc. If you're planning on having a garage sale, save everything you would normally throw away or give away when eliminating clutter from your household. This includes broken, old, and unusable stuff. You'll be surprised at what people will buy.

You can build up to your garage sale gradually. When cleaning closets, instead of a throwaway box (except for wastepaper or trash), keep a garage sale box at hand. Store the box and its contents someplace out of the way and place potential sales items in it. Eventually you'll begin to accumulate a considerable number of salable objects. It's easier to get rid of clutter knowing you will get something in return for it.

If you don't think you have enough things to sell, you can always get together with another family or two. You don't necessarily have to bunch the items together in one place, as long as you are near enough neighbors that people can drive up and walk around the separate displays.

You can do as much or as little preparation as you'd like. Tables for display, racks for clothes, and bags for purchased merchandise are all fine, but some people simply set their objects out on their carport and find that works just as well. It is a good idea to clean up your merchandise as much as possible, so that people aren't bargaining out the cleaning time from the price.

Signs are the best way to get people to your sale. Advertising is usually too expensive unless you have a full-scale selling operation going. Put clear, large signs with your address and bold words GARAGE SALE at the main streets near your home. Then post signs along the easiest route to your house. Look around your town, you'll find either Saturday or Sunday is the best time for garage sales.

Sticker labels are the best way to affix prices to your merchandise. Deciding what price to ask is more of a problem. Go to a couple of local sales to determine what prices merchandise is bringing in your area—it's the most efficient way to keep you from overpricing or underpricing your merchandise. Don't use the common pricing mechanism of pricing just under an even dollar. Price your merchandise in round numbers: $3, $3.50, even 25 cents. You'll avoid annoying buyers, and making change will be simplified.

The low-priced merchandise can be set out randomly on tables. More expensive objects should be kept near you or the cashier if you have one. You should have at least one other person at the sale to help you. If the sale becomes very busy, the cashier won't have to watch the crowd and make change at the same time.

Don't sell antiques. Leave that task to professionals. Merchandise you don't sell, throw away or donate to charity.

Studio or Small Apartments

A small apartment offers the greatest challenge to clutterers. Not only is there little space for storage, but almost every activity must be done in the same room.

Simply put, the lack of space can teach you quicker than anything else how to eliminate clutter from your life. The intensity of the space problem will help you decide whether something is truly necessary. You will get into the habit of going through your things yearly to cull out the old and unused and make room for the new. You will have to, or soon you won't have any space in which to move around. You'll learn to make your bed every morning because you never get away from it. It's make the bed or sleep on dirty sheets because you've been sitting on them all day.

The best way to live in a small apartment is to keep similar activities and possessions in the same area, eliminating the disorganization that leads to clutter. Designate areas for specific things; a table near the kitchen is the dining room. The desk is your office, but this can be further defined by putting the desk in a corner and blocking the view of the rest of the room by putting up a partition or bookcase.

Partitions come in handy in studio rooms, but don't abuse the idea. Your space is small already. If you chop it into tiny areas with partial dividers, you'll become claustrophobic. An alternative is a row of tall plants that cut visibility rather than eliminating it.

Storage should concentrate on moving high, with high shelves or cabinets built from the ceiling in your bathroom or a small nook in the room. Bookshelves should also go high. Keep a folding ladder handy or a footrest that can double as a ladder.

In a small apartment, furniture may become clutter. Decide which pieces of furniture you use most often, and eliminate the ones that take more space than they save in storage or use. You may have to replace your large desk with a small table and a file cabinet tucked under one side. Your large armchair might be replaced by two smaller chairs, creating a conversation nook. Remove the leaves from your dining room table to make it as small as possible, and store the leaves for dinner parties. Nesting tables are great in small apartments for holding projects or eating from the sofa.

The bed offers several possibilities. In a long room, it can be blocked off from the rest of the room by a hanging screen or curtain. If you like to watch television from bed, keep the bed exposed in the room, but add a cushion along the wall so that the bed can double as a couch.

A bed that opens out is not always as convenient as it appears to be, especially if it is the bed you regularly sleep in. The space taken when the bed is open may fill the room in an awkward way. Besides, it must be put away in the morning and opened at night, a time-consuming and sometimes complicated task for those who live busy lives. As a result, that convertible bed may stay out permanently if you aren't careful. A daybed that can double as a couch is often the best option. Or a trundle bed that pulls from a narrower daybed to join for a larger sleeping bed.

When you buy new furniture, get pieces that can double as storage spaces. An eating table may be supported by a cabinet at the base; an end table might have drawers or a cabinet underneath. A wall unit can organize quite a lot of stuff, including clothes, if it has drawers. Trunks can act as tables or seating, while footstools can have storage under the cushions. If you have deep windows, a cushioned window seat with storage underneath provides a fantastic storage item.

In a small apartment, it is very important to remember the "frames." Don't keep things around simply because you've found a place for them. This sort of niche filling eliminates the frames to your interior design and creates a sense of clutter in a small room. You may not have a large room, but you can create a sense of spaciousness in the way you arrange everything.

Also refer to Chapter 5, "Storage," for shelving and hanging suggestions.

9 | *Office and Desk Clutter*

When you are ready to begin working on a project, do you have to clean off your desk or work surface?

Is your desk crowded with objects or piles that are seldom used or referred to?

Do you think that a full desk indicates a busy and competent worker?

Your work environment should be the most efficient area of your life. Clutter is never more harmful than when it's in your office or on your desk. This chapter deals solely with your own work environment, offering organizing suggestions and tips on eliminating clutter.

Office

Use only one calendar to record appointments and deadlines, rather than listing work-related activities on one calendar and family events on another. When recording projects or events, include all the pertinent information on your calendar: time, telephone number, address, name and title of the person you're meeting, and directions if you need them.

For projects, you should put all your notes and ideas in one notebook, spiral or ring bound. Get a size that is comfortable to you. Write down in it all your ideas and information for individual projects so that pieces of paper don't become scattered throughout your desk or home.

If the notebook does appeal to you, consider forming an Idea file. You could create several Idea files; for creative work, for business or home-related projects. The goal is to create the habit of reaching for your notebook whenever you get ideas or information regarding your projects.

A bulletin board can also be used for revolving notes or ideas. Clean off the board once or twice a month to keep old numbers or notes from accumulating.

You should maintain a typed list of often-used phone numbers in your work area. Post the list over your telephone to make it as useful as possible. With a phone list, you simply glance up instead of having to thumb through your phone directory or Rolodex.

If you often refer to business cards you collect from colleagues and contacts, buy a business card holder. You can alphabetize the cards or place them in order of need. If you don't want to go to the trouble of sorting your business cards, file them in a folder for future reference. Some people like to keep their collected business cards in a box on their desk, but this is useless clutter. Your own business cards should be displayed in a holder on your desk, but other people's cards should be filed in folders according to where you will need them.

Desk

While organizing your work desk, remember that the people who have the cleanest desks are usually the bosses. The president's desk is seldom cluttered. Or left cluttered overnight. Just as you dress for success, have your office and desk dress for success.

So don't store things on top of your desk. The work space should be kept clear of everything except for the things you use every day. If you always use the Scotch tape dispenser, put it on top. If you don't, then keep it in a drawer.

Always have a trash can within reach of your desk. Throwing away papers and keeping your work surface clean is the best way to clear a path through the clutter that accumulates on your desk.

This includes knickknacks. If you must, have only one, or at most two, knickknacks (pictures, decorative objects, toys) on the top of your desk. Knickknacks are distracting, and where you work is not the place to be distracted. Besides, having a jumbled desk can convey a sense of disorganization, or tension and frustration that will be reflected in your work.

Clear off your desk every night after you are done working. When you come to your desk fresh the next morning, you won't spend your time rearranging things and putting files away. That's a sure opening for procrastination.

After you have cleared off the clutter, you will be able to determine if your desk is big enough for your needs. Often, even after the clutter is cleared away, the problem is simply that the desk is too small. Obtain a work surface to suit your needs. But remember this is not a license to store objects on your desk. The larger surface is for working.

Supplies

Make certain you have your supplies near your desk. It will keep you from having to get up and down while you're trying to work. Remember not to leave these items on the work surface, put them in a handy drawer instead. Suggested supplies to be kept handy:

- Plenty of file folders—the best are the three-quarter tab cut, so the labels can be staggered
- Labels and clear plastic tabs for the folders
- Pens and pencils—keep some on your desk in a pencil holder or tray, whichever suits you best
- Paper—in pads and loose bond
- Stationery and envelopes

Suggested equipment to be kept handy:

- Scissors, stapler, letter opener, staple remover, paper clips, pencil sharpener, rubber bands, ruler, Scotch tape, white-out,
- Dictionary
- Clock
- Calendar
- Phone directory
- Reference books
- Trash can
- Telephone and answering machine
- Two-drawer file cabinet.

Even if you have only one drawer worth of files, it is likely you'll expand your files over the years. Besides, that extra drawer makes a handy place to store your supplies.

10 | *Paper Clutter*

*When you're looking for a document, can you find it
in less than a minute?*

*Have you ever lost or misplaced an important
document?*

Does the daily mail create havoc in your life?

Eliminating paper clutter from your life only takes a
few simple, basic techniques. This chapter will focus
primarily on the routing procedures necessary to sorting
and handling documents and information.

Loose Paper

Stacks. More stacks. Stacks on stacks. Have you ever
caught yourself wondering what your desk looked like
underneath all those stacks of paper?

There are four ways to process a piece of paper:

- You can take Action (read, call or write a response).
- You can Refer the document on to someone else.
- You can File the document for later use.
- You can Throw Away the document.

The best way to deal with incoming documents is to

decide how to process each piece of paper as soon as you receive it. Though constant interruptions are the bane of cluttered time, you should have a folder or file for each of these four processes, and a document can be quickly tossed one of them until you have the time to deal with it.

Action

Documents which require Action can either be tossed together in a "To Do" folder, or if you prefer to do some preliminary sorting, divide the documents into separate folders labeled Read, Write, Call, Record, Gather Information, etc.

For more information on how to properly process those documents in the Read folder, see the Read Effectively section in Chapter 14, "Cluttered Time." For documents that require a telephoned response, see Telephone, also in Chapter 14.

For some people, a Record folder is unnecessary. Small pieces of paper with phone numbers or addresses can be immediately recorded in your phone directory or address book. Then throw away the slip of paper. If you keep a Rolodex and want to type the address, then put the slip of paper with other documents that you intend to write a response to. Other loose papers can be transferred to your calendar in the form of notes to yourself or appointments.

If you like having your Action documents visible, you can place the folders in a rack on top of your desk. The best method is a vertical rack with folders. Horizontal boxes or compartments are not as good since it is easy for you to rifle through the pile and ignore some documents while processing others. When you constantly see something, your mind after a while tunes out the information. You want to process the documents which need action, not ignore them.

So be vigilant. If you use several different folders to

hold your Action documents, they should be completely emptied at least once a day. If you don't receive enough documents to make this feasible, simply sort your incoming documents into the four main processes, then immediately deal with the Action pile.

Refer

If it is necessary to refer documents to someone else, the recipient's name should be clearly marked on either the document itself or on a "sticky" that is attached to the document. Your name and the reason for referral should also be included.

There are several ways to refer the document to the proper person. You can simply toss the marked referral documents in an outbox, and when it is full, you then sort and distribute. Or if you often have documents to refer, you can have separate outboxes labeled with the names of the people you usually refer documents to. If you are using this technique in your home, each member of your family should have a special place, either on their work space or in a common area, where documents or messages can be left for them.

File

Procedures on how to create and maintain a filing system are covered in Chapter 11, "Filing System."

Loose documents that are waiting to be filed can often be placed in holding folders (just as you can break down the Action pile into Read, Write, etc.). If the paper is business related, have a Business to File folder at the front of your business files and tuck the loose documents in that until you can individually file those documents. If it's personal, you can have a Financial to File folder, or an Information to File folder.

Beware of the danger in this practice, though. You must

keep an eye on these files so that they don't become enormous catchalls for your loose papers. File the papers in your File folders once a week, or if you have less paper, then once a month. But do it.

Throw Away

When in doubt, save all tax, legal, and financial documents. Otherwise, if it doesn't have a purpose in your life, throw away the document. Throw away duplicates and out-of-date information.

Resource information should always be thrown away if you haven't got a specific purpose in mind for it *now*. This is usually the hardest rule to follow for Information Collectors (see Chapter 2, "Collectors").

If you can't stand to throw away magazines or newspaper articles, create an Information Reference file where you can write down the name of the periodical, the date, the title of the article, and the subject. Every library keeps microfilm of past periodicals, and it's easy to find and copy this information if you discover you absolutely need it later.

Mail

Is mail part of your clutter problem? For many people, those neat envelopes are an easy thing to ignore—especially junk mail. They pile up in various places, adding to your clutter problem.

Sort the mail into piles for each person in your home or office. Each person should have a specific place where their mail is put.

Sort your own mail into magazines, large envelopes, junk mail, and first class. If you find you lose interest after the magazines and first class, then do the junk mail first. After all, that's usually a simple job of slicing the envelope open, then tossing it in the trash.

Process the mail into one of the four categories every day: Action, Refer, File, or Throw Away. If you don't process your mail, the next day it qualifies as clutter. It doesn't take long if you keep on schedule: it's only when the mail piles up that it becomes a real chore.

Throw Away

Get rid of most of your mail right after you look at it. Throw it away or recycle it, but don't keep that pamphlet about insurance if you don't plan on buying any in the near future. With mail more than anything else, throw away the document if you aren't sure. After all, tomorrow you'll get a fresh batch, and insurance notices will be coming to you for the rest of your life. The idea is to free up your environment now and get rid of that clutter.

If you get a large amount of mail, consider setting up a recycling box to put the waste envelopes and paper in. You can combine it with your old newspapers and save precious space in landfills while clearing up the clutter from your home.

Action

The Action pile includes the letters you need to write or telephone a response to, the magazines which you place in one pile for skimming through before reading (See Read Effectively in Chapter 14, "Cluttered Time"), change-of-address notices that you need to enter into your Rolodex or address book, appointment confirmations that should be recorded in your calendar, etc.

Make all your phone calls and write your letters during the same block of time immediately after sorting through the mail. That will ensure it gets done. At the same time, you can process any documents waiting in the Action box or file.

Refer

The Refer pile should be distributed to the correct person, either by placing a labeled Post-it on it and putting it in your outbox or by physically conveying it to the person or their normal mail drop area.

File

The File pile includes anything that does not need to be dealt with immediately: mail-order catalog, unpaid bills, memos, insurance policies, legal documents, etc.

If you file your correspondence, then do it right after drafting the response. The business correspondence should go in the folder usually labeled by company rather than an individual's name. Label your hanging folder or large, legal-sized folder by company name and insert several smaller manila folders labeled by individual inside.

For personal correspondence, most people find it easiest to file incoming letters into one folder for each year. If you get more personal correspondence than you can properly file in this manner, look through your folder and determine whether the bulk comes from two or three specific individuals. If this is the case, make a file for each person. Then you can also put any information regarding this person in the same file. If you use a hanging folder system, put two manila folders in the hanging folder, one for correspondence and the other for general information pertaining to this individual.

11 | *Filing Systems*

When you're looking for a document in your files, can you find it in less than a minute?

Have you ever lost the hard drive on your computer as well as all the documents it contained?

Does the idea of organizing your files make you cringe?

Filing systems are essential to keeping your records and information accessible. If you don't have an organized system, then you are probably surrounded by file clutter. This chapter will focus on how to create and maintain a filing system for both your paper documents and your computer documents.

Paper Filing

Start simply. If you don't have many files, then use a vertical system (racks) rather than piling your documents into stacks. Files also have a tendency to disappear in stacks, while racks display the folders. You'll be able to see which files are useful and which are not. The useless files are clutter and should be eliminated.

Medium-sized organizers include accordion folders and file boxes. Accordion folders can be very handy.

Some large accordion folders are labeled, or you can label them yourself. Accordion folders can be used year after year if you don't acquire many new documents, or you can use one accordion folder a year. If you are just starting a filing system, an accordion folder is perfect for organizing your documents.

If you have enough files for a filing cabinet, create a filing system that works for you. Be consistent. That is the only way you won't get lost in your own files.

Labeling Files

If you call your car a car, don't label the folder "Automobile." Also, don't label a folder with an individual's name if you're dealing with her company. Always label according to last name if you do have folders for individuals.

When filing information articles for future projects, don't file an article on cats under Cats if the project you're thinking of using it in is Veterinary Research. You can go to any library and look under Cats for helpful books and articles. In your personal filing system, articles and documents should be filed according to the function you plan on using them for. Think carefully about each piece of paper before filing it to make certain you are putting it in the place where it will do you the most good.

Make your files broad enough so that they can contain a number of articles and documents. You don't want to get into the habit of creating a new file for every new piece of information that comes across your desk.

You can also consider cross-referencing your files. Write a short description of the information and the folder it is filed in on a piece of paper. If you have a large filing system, this can be a lifesaver. Your Pension file can be under the Personal Category, but you may want its location noted in the Financial Category as well.

Organizing Your Files

All of your files should be alphabetized according to the label. Again, you must make certain the labels are easily recognizable, in the words that you most often refer to the file. You should be careful to refile your folders in their correct, alphabetical order.

You can break your files into manageable chunks by forming large categories so that, for example, the Taxes folder will not be alongside the Tour Guides folder in your filing cabinet. Folders within each category can then be alphabetized.

A few main categories are: Financial, Information, Personal, and Business. Each category can be color-coded to aid in refiling the folders, and the categories should be clearly marked within your file cabinet.

The following are some examples of files you are likely to need in each category.

Financial Files:
> Banking—savings, checking, credit cards
> Contracts
> Housing—rental agreements, mortgages
> Insurance
> Investments—bonds, stocks, real estate
> Loans
> Receipts, Warranties, Guarantees
> Taxes
> Unpaid Bills—utilities, rent, credit cards

Information Files:
> Bargains and Sales
> Consumer Information
> Coupons
> Decoration
> Entertainment
> Gift Ideas

Health and Beauty
Maps and Tourist Information
Restaurants
Services
Travel

Personal Files:
Automobile
Correspondence
Employment—résumé, pension
Hobbies
Medical History
School History

Business Files:
Contacts
Correspondence
Expansion
Insurance
Marketing
Personnel
Related Businesses
Vendors

Within each individual folder, often the best way to organize the information is by filing date. That is, consistently file your information from either the front of the back of the folder so that the papers are in chronological order of entry.

If you have certain files that you often use, color-code these in a fourth color and put them at the front of your file drawer. But don't use this method unless it is a case of ten folders that are used almost every day while the others are seldom referred to.

Maintaining Your Files

You should file your loose papers depending on the amount you receive each week. Should it be weekly or daily? Could you put it off to twice a month? Do whatever makes most sense, but stick to your system.

To make filing faster, after taking Action on a document (reading a letter or an article), indicate in pencil or on a Post-it the name of the folder in which the document should be filed. That way, you won't have to reread the document to determine where it should be filed.

Don't get in the habit of pulling files which you plan on using during a project. That's how files get lost and piles begin to form. Instead, write down the files you will need in your Ideas notebook. Or if you realize a letter should be written to someone, don't pull the file until you are ready to write that letter. Write it down as a reminder rather than using a pulled file to remind you.

Loose papers can wait to be filed, but folders should always be immediately refiled after you are done with them. That is the only way to keep your filing systems useful.

Storage Files

If your files grow quickly, you can maintain a limited number of current ones by jotting down the date on the outside of the folder every time you refer to a file. This will help you determine when a file should either be put in storage files or thrown away.

You should go through your filing cabinet once or twice a year and reexamine the contents. The files you seldom or never refer to should be carefully considered. Often the entire folder can be thrown out; if not, a large majority of the papers inside of it may be discardable.

Go through the folders you regularly refer to as well. There is no reason to keep every piece of paper in a folder simply because it's been filed. Throw out old articles that you have replaced with updated ones, duplicate articles, etc.

When a folder gets very full, go through it, cull the useless documents and throw them away, or put them in a new folder in the storage files.

If you are hesitating over throwing out a file, put it in your storage files. Only very important files, like taxes, financial information and legal documents, should go in storage. Doctors should store old client files for a certain number of years, just in case legal action ever ensues. Never put Information Files in storage.

Storage files can be placed in a less accessible part of your file drawer, or in boxes. Office supply stores sell sturdy boxes perfect for file folders.

Computer Clutter

If you own a computer, and suffer from paper clutter, it's likely you also suffer from computer clutter.

Your computer files should be kept as up-to-date as your paper files, otherwise, your computer will become cluttered. When your hard disk is full, the operation of your computer is slowed down and needed byte space is wasted.

If you've ever lost your hard disk, you've learned the hard lesson of backing up your documents to floppy every day after you've finished working on them. If you haven't, don't wait for disaster to strike before you learn to back up your files. Hard disks last for an estimated three to five years, but that doesn't mean they don't occasionally conk out after one year, or even six months. Get in the habit of backing up your files daily; it's easy once you start.

Organizing Computer Files

First, your software should be loaded in an organized manner. The root directory should not hold all the information; it should only have the access to each program. DOS, database, and your word processing software should each have its own subdirectories. Any DOS manual will give you step by step instructions on how to do this.

Within your word processor, you have access to subdirectories as well. Use these subdirectories to organize your files. Just as you have the Financial, Personal, Information, and Business categories in your filing system, you should use major categories as headings for your subdirectories. Don't create too many subdirectories or it will take a long time to travel between them.

If you work for several people, you can label a subdirectory for each person. If you write, you have subdirectories for Journal, Book, Poetry, Letters, etc. Work out a system that suits you best.

If the menu in each subdirectory is not large, simply leave the files in alphabetical order. If you have a full menu, you can arrange the files so that often-used files are at the top of the menu by putting "A-" or "1-" in front of the file name.

Storage Files

You should go through your files regularly, backing up and deleting obsolete files from your hard disk regularly, backing up and deleting obsolete files from your hard disk. You can use the same date-marking system whereby you type the date on the document screen prior to calling up the document every time you refer to that file. Then when checking the date, you can quickly call up the document screen (without having to load the entire document) to see whether the file has been recently used or not. If you haven't referred to a file lately, then transfer the documents to a floppy and clearly mark the contents on the label.

You should periodically evaluate subdirectories for continued usefulness, as well. If you find you don't use a subdirectory, then copy its contents to floppy and eliminate the entire subdirectory. If two subdirectories are similar and have small menus, then combine the two. This will save time traveling between subdirectories.

If you maintain the files in your computer in this manner, eventually you will acquire piles of floppy disks. Don't keep disks around for years. Just as you should occasionally go through your storage files to eliminate obsolete folders and documents, go through your floppies and format the obsolete files.

Remember to always keep financial, tax, and legal information. Save these files onto a new floppy labeled Tax, Financial, or Legal Info, along with the current date.

12 | *Financial Clutter*

*Have you received a disconnect or late notice in the
past year due to a mistake in paying the bills?*

*Would all your important documents be lost if your
file cabinet was destroyed?*

Though the visible signs of financial clutter are not as
striking as household clutter, it is the worst type of
clutter because it is much more important to your liveli-
hood. Losing your bills among the rest of your clutter can
result in disaster. This chapter deals with ways to organize your bills and financial information. It also deals
with the safety and storage of important documents.

Banking

Keep all your banking statements and deposit slips
together. Put these small slips of paper in a special place
in your purse or briefcase. File them in a Banking folder
as soon as you can, to prevent accumulation of clutter in
your carry bag.

Some banks have a service whereby they keep your
used checks for you for a certain length of time. This is a
good service if your canceled checks fill scores of boxes.

You don't actually need the check itself if you keep good records in your checkbook. Besides, the number and amount are included on your statement. Always save your banking statements, they are an important part of your tax information.

You should have a current list of your account numbers and the telephone number of the company in case you need to call. Usually there is a 1-800 telephone number for emergencies and replacements. Numbers you should have on file are:

- Bank accounts—savings and checking
- Credit cards
- Driver's license
- Social Security number
- Insurance policies
- IRAs
- Savings bonds
- Stock certificates

Bills

Plan on going over your bills once a week or, at the very least, once every two weeks. Don't do it once a month, because bills arrive at different times throughout the month, and payment dates will differ. By keeping up to date on your bills, you will avoid extra finance charges.

In separate folders, file your receipts, charge carbons, unpaid bills, and paid bills. This will cut down on the confusion that comes from jumbling everything together.

When you receive a bill, you should check your receipts against the charges to make sure they are correct. Don't assume that your bill is correct; sometimes very large mistakes can happen. Even in this age of computers, there remains the human error factor.

Put the date and policy or account number of the bill you are paying on your check and in the checkbook. This will ensure your records are up to date, and you will know instantly if you've been billed twice. Also, if a late notice comes, you'll be able to determine whether you paid the bill before or after the company sent the notice and can inform them of the date it was sent when you call.

On the part of the bill which you retain for your files, mark the date it was paid along with the amount. This is sometimes easier than keeping all the information in your checkbook.

Total the amount left in your account after every check. If you don't, you are likely to overdraw your account.

Safe Deposit Box

Everyone should have a safe deposit box in a bank. Anything valuable or irreplaceable should be put in this box. This includes:

Birth and marriage certificates
Divorce papers
Military discharge papers
A copy of your will
Pension plan
Titles to your cars, home, and other property (recreational vehicle, real estate, etc.)
Passports
Stock certificates, bonds, and certificates of deposit
Valuables, such as jewelry, heirlooms, coins, and stamps

Make certain you have a list of what your safe deposit box contains in a properly marked file. Then you won't have to visit the bank to discover whether your pension plan, say, is not in the box, but filed with your employment records.

If you would rather keep your valuable documents at home, invest in a strongbox or fireproof safe. Though this puts your important documents at your fingertips, this is not the best option, since a strongbox can be stolen and a safe can be broken into.

13 | *Priorities and Procrastination*

Do you have trouble deciding what should be done during your workday?

Do you often put off projects, only to have to rush to finish within the deadline?

You must take into account the characteristics of your own nature if they conflict with your desire for order. Indeed, time management systems are based upon assumptions that you are in control of your time. This chapter offers ways to formulate priorities and deal with procrastination.

Priorities

If you continually have days when you feel that you've accomplished nothing, then you aren't doing the important tasks.

If you can't readily define what is most important in your life, write down some options. Spell out your goals, both long- and short-term. This will help you decide the priorities in your life. It will also keep you from being confused by other people's suggestions of what should be important to you.

Things that further your primary goals present your most important tasks and therefore take priority over everything else.

To make certain you are doing the most important things, keep track of your plans, tasks, lists, appointments, and activities. If you need to keep track of both work and home, the best solution is a small daily or weekly calendar. Often these calendars have places for long- and short-term goals as well.

It is not a good idea to separate work and private activities or to keep both an appointment book and a calendar. A calendar is supposed to help you be organized, and having to cross-reference two calendars makes this system less efficient and more time consuming. Though the two-page desk calendar is good for lists, it is stationary at work or on your desk. Some people prefer to use large, erasable calendars. These suit families especially well.

Work with your calendar system until it suits your needs, then make a habit of writing down everything you must remember. Don't rely on memory alone; this will not provide the objectivity you need to decide what is most important. With an up-to-date calendar, it is easy to form your daily, weekly, and monthly schedule.

At the beginning of each year when you buy your new calendar, go through the old calendar and transfer important dates to the new one.

Procrastination

People procrastinate for all sorts of reasons. You need to evaluate each situation to determine what is causing your hesitation. Sometimes, all you need do is recognize a certain pattern in order to form new habits. Following are some new tips to try when you find yourself faced with a project that you just can't seem to get started on.

Manipulate Time

One simple trick often works. Record the due dates of projects and appointments on your calendar as a little earlier than they actually are. If you have a meeting at 1:00, record the time as 12:45. If a report is due Monday, note that it is due Thursday or Friday.

Even though you may remember that you have a few extra days or minutes, the psychological impact of seeing an earlier date will help speed you along. Also, try telling yourself that the early time is correct. Forget you have extra time. This will keep you from delaying the start of your project until the weekend before it's due.

A similar method is to set arbitrary deadlines for yourself. Tell yourself that you must write that letter by Thursday, or by eight this evening. You'll be amazed how it works, especially if you have a fairly good helping of guilt in your nature.

Render the Task Into Smaller Pieces

Break down large projects. It's easier to face a score of little tasks than one enormous job. It won't take less time, but if your problem is procrastination, you may be able to trick yourself into doing several of the small tasks before you realize it. Then you're a third of the way through your large project.

Sometimes all it takes is one movement forward to break the barrier of procrastination. Find the easiest part of the task and begin with that. It doesn't matter if that particular task does not need to be completed until the end of the project. Just as directors shoot films with the scenes out of sequence, many unwieldy tasks can also be handled in the same manner.

Don't wait for a huge block of time to do the entire project. If you have to organize your library, do whatever can be done in little blocks of time. If the project will take weeks or months to complete, you may need to break it into sections before you start, so that you allow yourself a series of successes in the smaller tasks rather than waiting for the completion of the project. These small successes also give you a second wind for the next stage of the project.

Stop Being a Perfectionist

Sometimes your standards are too high. If that makes a task seem overpowering, you may never get around to doing it. Don't aim to be perfect: aim to get the job done. If you are a perfectionist, then figure your habits of polishing the work will kick in later. Don't think about perfection at the beginning or you will frighten yourself right out of the running.

If you can't take a step for fear of going in the wrong direction, don't worry. Take that step anyway. Just as most writers throw away the first page, or first chapter, of a piece, often the preliminary steps are needed for you to realize what direction you need to go in.

Sometimes, the only thing you can do is give in to the inevitable. If you must procrastinate, don't do anything else for at least fifteen-minutes. Don't read, don't talk to anyone, don't take phone calls. After a few minutes of simply thinking about that project waiting for you, you'll do anything to get it going.

Unpleasant Tasks

Sometimes people procrastinate because a particular task is unpleasant. From childhood you learn that if you ignore things you don't like to do, someone eventually comes along and does it. Or else you are forced by an adult to do it. This creates a terrible pattern in which you rely on someone else to get you to work. Ask yourself if this is your problem and then become your own adult figure.

Whenever possible, delegate tasks you don't like to do. That will ensure that they get done while at the same time freeing you from the task.

If you must do an unpleasant task, reward yourself when you have finished. Take a fifteen-minute break, go for a walk around the block, treat yourself to a snack. The carrot of reward almost always works better than the stick of punishment. Even if you'd never think of rewarding yourself, try it when you're faced with a daunting task.

Is there one type of task on which you regularly procrastinate? If so, the problem could be related to the work environment. Perhaps when you have to write letters, your typing equipment is hard to set up. Or when you have to pay bills, the phone rings constantly. What you consider to be a difficult task could result from surroundings that interfere with performing that task.

Look Beyond the Task

If nothing works to get you started, perhaps there are deeper reasons for your procrastination. Ask yourself why you haven't written to your mother-in-law or called the travel agent about vacation plans. The simplest tasks can sometimes be fraught with the greatest emotional tension. Coming to terms with that tension may be more important than getting the task done—and it may be the only way it gets done.

14 | *Cluttered Time*

Have you recently forgotten an appointment or meeting?

Do you suffer from constant interruptions, either from the phone or from people dropping by unexpectedly?

Do you often cover the same ground two or three times when running errands?

Cluttered time is the inability to organize your activities, your schedule, and your life. Your time is affected by the way you approach your tasks and the systems you use for completing them. This chapter will focus on the time-managing systems which you can use to organize your activities.

Time Management

Many people who let clutter invade their life are also harassed by cluttered time. If you constantly swing from procrastination to frantic activity, then your time is cluttered. If you are always late or forgetting the things you need for your day, then you have to organize your time.

Organizing your time involves decisions, just as getting rid of clutter requires decisions. You can't have hassle-free time without making a few rules for yourself. Time management is using the right tools and habits to improve the way you perform a task.

Double Up on Time

Constructively use the time you spend commuting or standing in lines. Go through your bills, read a good book, write a letter. Double up your time—do your mending while talking on the phone, or exercise while watching television. Combine errands—pick out a birthday card while you're going to the bank, or take your shoes to be fixed while getting the paper.

Get into car pools, whether it's for yourself or your child's gymnastic lessons.

Plan Ahead

When you begin a project, think of the tools and resources you will need. Gather everything together in one place that has a proper work surface. Don't start something without the proper tools or information, or you will just have to stop at some crucial point.

Carefully consider how much time this project will take, and determine exactly when and how long you will work at a time. Don't jump from one project to another; that wastes time. If it's a small project, like writing a letter, finish it before moving on to the next task.

Have a clock in every room to avoid the excuse of not knowing the time. Set the clocks ahead a few minutes, but no more than that or you'll start compensating in your head.

Keep Records

Don't try to keep records in your head. Use the resources you have to write down appointments and ideas, as well as information you hear or read. Recording everything will save you from making mistakes that could easily be avoided.

Don't let your record-keeping become note clutter. Appointments should be recorded on your calendar, with backups if necessary on a bulletin board. Information, ideas, and conversations should be noted and filed in the proper folder. This will keep your mind free for processing the information rather than simply trying to remember it.

Create Forms

Preprint or type labels for frequently used addresses. Use forms for information gathering or delegating, such as Self-Addressed Stamped Postcard confirming reservations and appointments, cards to accompany FYI information (I think you will find this interesting, Please call ASAP, or No response necessary, with a box to check which action you prefer). Also, forms for children's field-trip permission, and requests for prices or terms with a space for the company's name.

Create form letters if large parts of your correspondence are similar. Collect letters that you receive that are particularly effective and file them in a Sample Letters file. Create and regularly update your form letters based on these sample letters. Preprinted address labels or a stamp will help speed up your mail processing. Use window labels whenever possible to save typing the address.

Read Effectively

Learn to skim rather than read. The first and last paragraph, and the first sentence of each paragraph can tell you quickly if this article is something you truly want to read. Reports, memos, letters, almost anything can be skimmed to garner the pertinent information, then processed by placing in piles for Action, Referral, Filing, or Throw Away.

When faced with large amounts of material to be read, skim through the periodicals and rip out any article that you find interesting or important. From a large stack, you will end up with a small pile. It is psychologically reassuring to see a much smaller stack of reading than to be faced with a huge stack of periodicals.

You should have a permanent place in your purse or briefcase for these skimmed articles or letters to be read. The much smaller stack is easy to carry and can be read while commuting or waiting on hold on the telephone or during any odd moment. Once you've read them, discard them.

For some people, setting up a specific time during the day to read works beset. If you can stick to this schedule, fine. But for most, especially those having a problem with cluttered time, odd bits of time are easier to deal with and often are adequate for reading needs.

Be sure to cancel subscriptions that are no longer important or useful. This will eliminate some clutter before it reaches you.

Services

For any unpleasant or time-consuming chore, professionals are available to undertake the task for a fee. Look into errand-runners if you are short on time.

Pay to have servicemen come in the morning or after work if you don't want to take time off. Many hairstylists or manicurists will make house calls, and there are veterinary services that come to your door to give your pet its annual shots.

Take advantage of the pickup and delivery services

offered by many merchants. Groceries can be bought once a week if they are delivered to your door. Laundry, drug stores items, and take-out food can all be delivered.

If you don't like housework, hire someone to come in one afternoon or one day a week to do it. Go over the house carefully with your cleaner and decide what your priorities are.

Interruptions

Most interruptions are caused by conflicting priorities, when what you want to do collides with what someone else is doing, and that creates cluttered time.

You should plan for the fact that there will be interruptions in your life. Always give yourself extra time to finish that important project by recording the due date as earlier than it is or by blocking out a third more hours than you think you'll need.

Note interruptions, such as new information, ideas, and changes that need to be made in your Ideas Notebook, then put it aside until later. As much as possible, continue with the project at hand and clean up interruptions at a later time.

Work

Ask friends or colleagues to give you notice before dropping by. Better yet, set certain hours when you are free to speak to people.

Consolidate appointments or visitors into a set time. If someone just drops by, you can instruct him or her to come at a later time. Soon everyone will become accustomed to the times you are available.

If you find you are continually being interrupted by people who work for you, perhaps you are not fully explaining their tasks or providing them with all the necessary information when you assigned a project. Keep this in mind when you next delegate tasks and try to quickly cover all contingencies. You'll then only be bothered when a true crisis occurs rather than by each small question. Also, if possible, make your files accessible to your employees so they can answer their questions for themselves.

If you find the same sort of questions keep being rerouted to you, make up a master list with sample solutions to common problems. This can save you a lot of time in the long run.

Family

You should also teach family members to respect your work hours or private time. Let them know when you do not want to be interrupted, either by designating set hours for private time or by using a DO NOT DISTURB sign.

If your family continually interrupts your private time, determine their most frequent types of requests. Do they want food? Or do they want help with something? Try to anticipate the problems and solve them before they arise. Set up convenient snack foods for children and arrange for homework hours during which you will be free to help them.

Mornings

If you aren't your best in the morning, clear the clutter out of your way the night before.

Lay out your clothes before you go to sleep. You won't waste time in the morning figuring out what you want to wear. You will also know if a button needs to be sewn on or whether your shoes are scuffed.

Set the breakfast table the night before. Put the cereal or bread on the counter and make sure the coffee machine has a filter and coffee in it ready to be turned on. You can do this when you clean up from supper the night before, combining your preparations with cleanup in the kitchen.

Pack your purse or briefcase the night before. Go over your calendar to make certain you have everything you need for the next day.

Have one place where your keys are kept; that way you will never misplace or lose them. The easiest solution is to buy a key board to hang right beside the door (see Chapter 5, "Storage"). Have one table near the door where you put the odd items you'll need to take with you, such as theater tickets or dry cleaning.

If you're especially disorganized in the mornings, put everything you'll need together. With hat, coat, gloves, shoes, keys, purse, and briefcase in one place near the front door, you won't forget anything.

Set up a morning routine. Make the bed immediately. For some people, that can be an impossible habit to acquire. But work on it. Once it's a habit, you never have to think about it again.

Children and Time

A large monthly calendar with everyone's schedule clearly marked is the biggest help for organizing family time. Mark down doctor's appointments, sports practices and games, Scout meetings, music lessons. Birthday parties, school conferences, sleep-overs, and special events should also be recorded.

If you don't want to maintain a large calendar, have a special place for school items for yourself and your children—a bulletin board for posting lunch schedules, field trips, due dates, and projects.

Telephone

Your phone area should be clear of other paperwork. This provides you with a free surface for whatever you might need to do while on the phone. Always take notes while on the phone. Note taking will save your having to call back to check on something you learned during a conversation.

Do most of your phone work in advance. Prepare the information you will need to supply and have it handy before making the call. Also, compose the questions you'd like to ask and be ready to write the answers down.

If phone calls constantly interrupt your work, set aside a certain block of time when you will be free to take calls. Get an answering machine and screen your calls. Return all phone calls during a specific time period rather than responding to each one separately.

Unplugging the phone can be your best move sometimes. Of course, if you must be accessible twenty-four hours a day, then this is not feasible. But do you really have to be accessible at all times? Can't you turn off the phone for a half hour while you nap or finish a project so that the ring or answering machine won't wake you up?

Learn how to end phone conversations effectively. For example:

- Refer to the main question or problem of the conversation. "Well, let me look into this and I'll get back to you."
- Segue into information that you need to call someone else soon or have to go to a meeting. "This is very interesting and I'd like to talk about it more, but I have to leave for my carpool soon."
- Sprinkle reminders in your sentences that the conversation will be ending soon. "All right, let's make sure we have this straight before we hang up."

- End the call if it starts to drag on. Usually the person who makes the call should end it. "Great, now that we have that cleared up, I guess we're okay. I'll talk to you again soon."

Make more outgoing calls. This should diminish incoming calls. Then you can prioritize your phone calls.

When you take a message, read back the information to eliminate mistakes. When you leave a message, have the person read back your name and phone number so that you know it's been taken down carefully and accurately.

When you leave a message for someone, specify a bracket of time when you will be available for a return call. That will prevent your having to phone again if the person should return your call while you are busy elsewhere.

Talking on the phone is a perfect time to do many small chores. Buy an attachment that allows you to reset the receiver on your shoulder for comfortable, no-hands talking. Or invest in a speakerphone. Then you can make notes, cook or cut vegetables, do simple housekeeping while talking on the phone. Have long extension cords on your phones so you are not tied to one spot.

Summary of Time Management

1. Unite similar activities so you cover the ground only once. When running one errand, do others at the same time: while standing in line, read articles.
2. Plan activities. Decide how much time should be allotted to each task. Explain possible solutions to problems for delegated tasks. Arrange a morning routine.

3. Record activities. Provide a place for children who go to school. You should also have a multiuse calendar for your work and home appointments.
4. Set up systems for repetitive tasks: use form letters and preprinted forms and labels.
5. Delegate activities. Children should help with chores. Merchants should come to your home. Assign projects to employees for submission for your approval.
6. Set up specific times during which you will be free for interruptions, at home or work, and by friends, colleagues and family.
7. Gain control of your phone calls. Make more calls than you accept, learn how to end long calls, be clear and concise while on the phone, and prepare your questions in advance.

Index